NORTH OF EDEN

ALSO BY RENNIE McQUILKIN

NORTH OF EDEN

New & Collected Poems

Fell 'The Fall' → Became human
Innocence → Experience

Eve Adam

Prelapsarian
Postlapsarian

* metafiction
– writing about writing)

rebirth

Rennie McQuilkin

Antrim House

Simsbury, Connecticut

Library of Congress Control Number: 2017935213

ISBN: 978-1-943826-25-4

First edition, 2017

Author photograph by Hunter Neal, Jr.

Front cover, pp. iii and xxi: Adam and Eve expelled from the Garden
of Eden: stained glass window in the Cathedral of
St. Michael and St. Gudula, Brussels, Belgium
(courtesy of Alamy, Ltd, UK)

Antrim House
21 Goodrich Road
Simsbury, CT 06070
860-217-0023
antrimhouse@comcast.net
www.antrimhousebooks.com

CREDITS & ACKNOWLEDGMENTS

Of the new poems herein, "October Flight," "A Brief History of the Skunk Cabbage," and "Hands" have appeared in journals: respectively in *Freshwater* (2014), *CT Woodlands* (Winter, 2017), and *Laureates of Connecticut* (2017). Poems collected from earlier books first appeared in a variety of journals and magazines: *The Atlantic, Poetry, The Yale Review, The Hudson Review, The Southern Review, The American Scholar, Crazyhorse, The Gettysburg Review, The Malahat Review, The Ontario Review, Poetry Northwest, Chelsea, The Kansas Quarterly, The Beloit Poetry Journal, MARGIE, College English, Prairie Schooner, Southwest Review, The Southern Poetry Review, Tar River Poetry,* and other publications.

The following publishers issued books in which poems from this collection originally appeared, often in earlier versions: The Texas Review Press (*An Astonishment and an Hissing*); Bauhan Publishing, Inc. (*North Northeast*); Swallow's Tale Press (*We All Fall Down*); and Antrim House — *Counting to Christmas, Learning the Angels, Passage, Private Collection, Getting Religion, First & Last, North Northeast* (2nd edition), *Visitations, The Weathering, Going On,* and *A Quorum of Saints*. Some of the poems in this collection have been anthologized in *Contemporary New England Poetry: A Sampler,* Volumes I and II (Texas Review Press); *Joyful Noise: An Anthology of American Spiritual Poetry* (Autumn House Press); *The Autumn House Anthology of Contemporary American Poetry; The Hungry Ear: Poems of Food & Drink* (Bloomsbury USA); *The Hampden-Sydney Poetry Review Anthology; Writing for Many Roles* (Boynton/Cook Publishers, Inc.); *Anthology of Magazine Verse & Yearbook of American Poetry* (Monitor Book Co., Inc.); and *Voices in the Gallery*.

"An Astonishment and an Hissing" was awarded the Ruth Fox Award of the Poetry Society of New England, judged by Helen Vendler, and was part of a chapbook by the same title, which received the Texas Review Chapbook Prize. *We All Fall Down* won the 1986 Swallow's Tale Poetry competition, judged by David Bottoms. "Ceremony, Indian Summer" won First Prize in the 1999 *Yankee* poetry competition. "Skunk Cabbage" was broadcast nationally in 2001 as part of National Public Radio's *Weekend Edition,* and "The Digging" was read by Garrison Keillor on *The Writer's Almanac*. In 2010 *The Weathering* was awarded the Connecticut Center for the Book's annual poetry award under the aegis of the Library of Congress. In 2006 the same group awarded McQuilkin a Lifetime Achievement Award, and in 2015 he was named Poet Laureate of Connecticut.

Special thanks to the National Endowment for the Arts and the State of Connecticut for their fellowships.

FOREWORD

North of Eden presents over two hundred poems not included in *The Weathering: New & Selected Poems* (2009). It offers new work written during the past eight years as well as much revised verse from previous books. It is the product not just of an elusive Muse but of those who have abetted me as a poet for years, most of all my wife Sarah, who has shared many of the moments recorded in the poems and has offered much useful criticism. My poet mother, Eleanor McQuilkin, was my first mentor. Without her example and encouragement I would never have scribbled a line. Nor would I have left my poetry closet without the encouragement and assistance of my ten splendid workshop colleagues: Steve Foley, Pit Pinegar, Pamela Nomura, Hugh Ogden, Emily Holcombe, Elizabeth Kincaid-Ehlers, Drew Sanborn, David Holdt, Susan Lukas, and Charles Darling. Many others have been generous with their support and criticism, especially Norah Pollard, Nancy Fitz-Hugh Meneely, Katharine Carle, Bessy Reyna, Robert Cording, Chivas Sandage, and Laura Mazza-Dixon. My thanks to you all and to so many others whose spirits speak through the poems in *North of Eden*. Finally, I thank Gray Jacobik, Eamon Grennan, and Richard Wilbur for their encouragement and gracious endorsements of the shorter volume of New & Selected Poems that preceded this book.

Rennie McQuilkin
Simsbury, CT

TABLE OF CONTENTS

II. REFUSAL TO MOURN

III. CHILD'S GARDEN

THE WEATHERING

I. MORNING

II. ORDINARY ANGELS

III. SUDDEN WEATHER

IV. WE ALL FALL DOWN

V. THIS

VI. MORE THAN I AM

VII. SMALL LIFE RISING

VIII. BESTIARY

PASSAGE

LEARNING THE ANGELS

AN ASTONISHMENT AND AN HISSING

COUNTING TO CHRISTMAS

NORTH NORTHEAST

AFTER THE FALL

Looking back at the angel
barring the entry to the Garden,
(we) held hands, got *dressed* next day
for *work*, considered what to (plant) → *future*
in a lesser garden. . . *responsibility*)

North of Eden the crops no longer grow
themselves, nor do the ewes birth safely
alone, and love no longer blooms
of its own accord. We are learning
to pay attention.

NORTH OF EDEN

APOLOGIA FOR POETRY

[handwritten: Apology / fight in favor of]

[handwritten: comparing Arts]

But why poetry? *[handwritten: life changing]*
Why not Woody Allen's latest? *[handwritten: entertaining]*

Nothing against Woody Allen.
I'm a fan.
But even *his* films are too paved
for this country boy, *[handwritten: straight foward / interpertation]*

[handwritten: choice?]

[handwritten: Metaphor] not like poetry's unkempt meadows
full of weeds with those names *[handwritten: Many different interpertations + meanings]*
I can never get enough of
(*Bridal Creeper, Corky Passionflower,*
St. John's Wort, Snakeweed). *[handwritten: unique]*

Most of all I relish the dark space
in poetry, rabbit holes one might
fall into and not be seen for days.

[handwritten: before reading Vs After reading]
[handwritten: Prelapsarian   Postlapsarian]

[handwritten: ✳ Metafiction]

NEW POEMS

I. RISING UP

ADAGIO

Maundy Thursday, my numb feet just bathed by the priest,
driving home beneath an Easter moon already waning,
lopped and blurred in mist, the FM also fading, I hear
through crackling static the story of the *Adagio in G Minor* —

how after the bombing of Dresden, a bass line and six bars
by Tomaso Albinoni were found among the charred ruins
of the Dresden State Library; and how from such measures
Remo Giazotto constructed the sadly beautiful *Adagio,*

not the sonata Albinoni had planned but an apt response to
Allied bombers destroying that *Florence on the Elbe* to avenge
the leveling of Coventry Cathedral; and how during the dark days
when Sarajevo was shelled to rubble to purify another people,

the *Adagio* was played in churches, mosques and synagogues,
their ruins still smoldering, by Vedran Smailović, his cello
completing what Albinoni began and what we hope to go on
celebrating in the ruins of civilization smoking all around us.

HIS VERY HEIGHT

for Susan Finnegan

She works to relieve her anguish —
hammers together the pine "stretchers,"
lays out the canvas, pulls it tight,
staples it down, inserts the hickory keys
at the corners, presses them in
to adjust the tension,

then applies layers of gesso, thinned
to vellum for the acrylics
to come, the part she puts off, puts off
until she can breathe
steadily enough to do what she must.
Between the coats of gesso, she washes
the brushes clean,
each bristle — a modus vivendi,

and learns all there is to learn
about the trees she will paint, the trees
he loved. She says their names aloud,
names like all the selves of him:

Bristlecone Pine
Ponderosa Pine
Colorado Blue Spruce
Piñon Pine
Lodgepole Pine
Rocky Mountain Juniper
Douglas Fir
Engleman Spruce
Grand Fir

Limber Pine . . .

Breathe. It is time to begin
filling in the 22 canvases she has stretched,
painting one tree on each for each of his years
before he snowboarded through his beloved
pine and firs and spruce

and soared off a cliff.
She will not have him come down
as he did, will paint him into the trees –

trees in the salmon, pink, magenta hours
of morning, trees in the golding hours,
evening trees flaring rose to
violet, purple, indigo,
trees in the blue hour
fading slowly

deep green to black. Pine, fir, spruce
trunks, limbs, branches, twigs
seen from above, beside, below,
directly, obliquely, opaquely –

trees urging always upward, outward,
implicit with him.
Trees.

She turns her grief to 22 tall canvases
his very height, very width,
22 tall canvases containing him
ascending.

ON THE ROTTING OF APPLES

You know how windfall apples
wrinkle, shrink, get gnawed by grubs,
ferment, send wasps into drunken whirligigs,

and rot away over winter
until they're down to slick black seeds
preserved by their own arsenic

nestling in spring mud and with any luck
beginning to root.
That's how some of us are feeling.

We old timers hope to grow
our spirits sufficiently to incite
a perfectly drunken thing or two

and if conditions are right
and our spirit seeds strong enough,
we'll take root

as something else –
a mouse, a barn owl, a great grandchild –
and rise up to drink the sun again.

EASTER SATURDAY

for Katharine Carle

Now a congregation of *Crucifers* is warming up
in the bog, and larger frogs in deeper water
fifty feet to the east of them have just now
begun to babble like Holy Rollers.

They see nothing the least bit ecclesiastical
in all of this. And I can't blame them. But that
won't keep me, nor will my disbelief, from
Easter thinking. I see the stone rolled into place,

the Roman guards settling down to sleep by it
and above, white wings singing, about to make
their move. Call them merely Judean skylarks
circling before their earthward dive, scarcely

angels, and I'll believe you, but only in the front
of my wisely credulous brain, for the season is
upon me. Death is in retreat. I'm just back from
visiting my childhood home. I have seen him,

dead for thirty years, in the place where his
wide, large-knuckled hand guided my small one
gently – to carve my initials in the wet concrete
of a footing just poured in November of 1940.

I have seen. The date is clear, the initials still
crisp, his warm hand steady, pressing its print
into mine. I believe in Resurrection.

BEING BEN

"If you get caught in lightning," said Lee Trevino,
"just hold up a 1 iron. Not even God could hit it."
But Ben Hogan could, and there's a plaque at Marion
to show where he stiffed one
sixteen months after being labeled dead-on-arrival.
He went on to win that major and many more.
Today the players leave divots all around his plaque,
but none of them can quite repeat the shot.

Where is Ben? Does he hear the roar of the crowds
as Tiger seriously sinks a 60-footer and pumps his fist,
counts his wins, and aims to 1-up the Golden Bear?
Ben won't descend, but I do believe he's hovering,
waiting to make a statement on the Golf Channel.
Another comeback.

A few years after the first, I saw him hook a 3-wood
(he called it by its proper name, the *Spoon*)
around a grove at Oak Hill, land it on the apron,
then limp to the fairway on his bum leg, lightning
shooting through it. The torque of hitting that hook

was enough to set him floating
overhead, as once he'd floated over his Caddy
wrapped around the bumper of a Greyhound
on an ice-slick, foggy morning,
February 2, 1949, pinned against the dashboard,
having thrown himself in front of Valerie.

From his new height, he looked down on #13
as if from the Goodyear blimp, watched

with bemusement as his namesake sank the putt.

That's how we old-timers are: ungrounded.
People stare at us, amazed we're still walking
the earth, which of course we aren't, appalled
by a hybrid world in which a "wood" is not a wood.
We look down from 1950 or so – about the time
Ben hit that Driving Iron to the 18th.
Jesus, what a beauty!

OCTOBER DANCE

an imperfect sonnet

At four score she cuts a fine figure 8 in this field of clover,
delighting in a pair of late-year dragonflies engaged
apparently in yoga, abdomens curled to form almost a cloven
heart, almost a circle. Preoccupied, wings transparently jade,
they allow her to memorize them, head turned by such elation
under an almost completed round of day moon seeding the sky
like the lacy white umbel of an October dandelion.
At the meadow's edge among its other autumnal celebrations,

a model biplane circles a boy aiming his remote like a wand.
She remembers: a toy helicopter, gyring down, severed
an artery in its owner's neck last month. This sobers her,
elevates the gracious stay she's been granted.
Once again she completes the slightly lopsided 8 of her trek,
horizontal pair of imperfect aughts with no beginning or end.

DANCE

For elders
with legs all but gone
and backs bent like wickets,
dancing can be dangerous.
Think of aging Isadora
in Nice, standing to twirl
in an open Amilcar Racer,
her gorgeous lavender scarf
flowing out behind her
sinking in a downdraft
and catching in those silver
spinning spokes,
just like *that*
breaking her beautiful neck.

But think too of King David,
his numb feet remembering
the naked caper he cut
to welcome Jehovah's Word
come out of hiding
and jouncing in an Ark
along the flower-strewn
streets of Jerusalem.

Today, dance is his salvation.
He dares the young to try
deposing him
where they wait outside
the royal chamber, listening
to see if he is able
to *know* the belly-dancing
Shunammite. He steals a tassel

from her glitter, gives
the laughing girl her end of it,
takes his own in one hand, timbrel
in the other, and shuffles into
a Sumerian Wedding Dance . . .
Today, the King must not die.

AFTER THE FIRST HARD FROST OF FALL

*In late fall, a strange blossoming of many plants occurs, along with court-
ship displays and singing of many species, frogs not least among them.*

Last night the *Crucifers*, those out-of-season frogs,
revived their courtship song before the front came through,
salvation of voice beneath the blue and sharpening shadows
of the Hunter Moon, the world leaning away from the sun.

This morning – silence, the ferns keeled, black and copper,
the remaining tomato and eggplant greens silver with rime.
O sing again, you autumnal frogs, and whistle your wings,
October doves – reprise again the ceremony of spring,

a music for the sake of music, no future in it, no brood,
just the joy of throat-swelling, wing-whistling song
despite or because of the end of things.

I am thinking of the Straus brothers in Vienna composing
victorious waltzes after so much loss in the Battle of Sadowa
when the Prussians widowed thousands of Viennese wives,
scattering parts of the young and handsome on the field

like the red debris of fall, fit only to be reassembled
in makeshift coffins shipped back to a mourning city draped
black, all commerce stopped, all joy suspended. The response

of the Strauses was *The Blue Danube* and more

rivers of music reviving a grieving city,
celebrating the dance of life. Oh you frogs and toads,
may we all carouse no less, however brief our waltz.

FINISH LINE

Yesterday, runners at the marathon's finish line
lost all or parts of themselves. The bombs were aimed
low – to explode their legs. There is a picture
of a runner, arms up, chest breaking
the finish line. To one side of him is the smoke
of an explosion. Too many others were just behind.

Last night I said poems at a retirement home.
Some of the audience came with double canes,
some in wheelchairs, some looking lost.
They were close to the finish line.
This morning I keep my eyes shut against the things
of this world an open window lets in: rapid firing

of ammunition being tested at Ensign Bickford,
the automatic weapon of a Pileated on the dying ash.
But listen – he's feasting or excavating a nest, and there
is a Phoebe repeating *FEE-be fee-BE FEE-be fee-BE* . . .
as if to assure himself he is. He is and he is and he is
ad nauseam I'd say, if I were not so delighted with him.

I am considering the brilliant and the subtle colors
the birds present, no flag-waving or flagging spirits
about them. I am opening my eyes,

I am lifting one leg out of bed, then the other.
I am feeling a little life in them beneath the new
numbness I have learned to live with.
Everything is questionable
this morning — and much more precious.

NOCHEBUENA

2003. Another Gulf War. We chant against it,
hold up our small lights, candles in paper cups
an otherworldly glow down the row of us
lining the sidewalk,
asking traffic from The Hartford and Travelers
to sound their horns in support. In vain.

I long for another age when paper cups,
the string stretched tight between them, meant
speaking privately into the echo chamber of one,
hearing the answer coming in a sound wave
down the line from the other. I found peace in
that, entrusted my secrets to such a phone.

Disconnected, I'm less and less where I am . . .
It's quickly 1970. I'm fleeing the country
while napalm and Agent Orange burn 'Nam,
fleeing to celebrate Christmas in Mexico,
a separate peace right down to the ripe red
pomegranate seeds served up by Aeromexico.

Then the inn in Cuernavaca, a walled garden,
no serpents allowed. Tree-high poinsettia
line one wall of the enclave; purple bougainvillea

leans from window boxes everywhere; the flower
beds are as lush as the town itself is desiccated,
its shanties hobbled along the deeply rutted streets.

Our children are enchanted by so much attention
lavished by the staff, which at least has work
unlike the desperate in town. There is no revolution
yet, though it will come, and the drug lords, the killings.
Still, all that is in the future.

For Christmas Eve, Angel, one of the cooks, invites
our children to walk with his own and their friends
in a "Posada." At the corner of Juventino and Del Sur
we find them holding candles,
their faces lit from below, full of the wonder
of American guests and tonight's search for an inn.

We all set off down Juventino, adults remembering,
children chanting *Ora pro nobis,* Pray for us,
each a little Joseph or Mary
searching for a place to spend the night. We go
from doorway to doorway, are told at each
No hay albergue en la posada — No room in the inn,
until we come to the chosen house,
this year's *posada.* The gate is thrown open,

and in the small courtyard a señora is grilling
tortillas for us. From a stunted jacarandas
a white, star-shaped piñata hangs. When a broomstick
is not enough to break it open, a burly young man
swings a sledge and the star explodes,
spraying a rain of red candy on the courtyard cobbles
to the delight of the children, who go to their knees,
collecting it in a frenzy.

Filled with history, I see too much
in a star exploding on Christmas Eve — an end of light,
flowering of cluster bomb flak in a Da Nang market,
medics down on hands and knees
among the parts, saving what they can.

Meanwhile the children are giddy with joy,
some of which returns to me at the midnight
mariachi service in the cathedral. Guitars, trumpets,
accordions, cymbals, castanets, drums
invite the Child to be born. When it's time for
the *abrazo*, an ample mestiza takes me in her arms.
I return the blessing.

At midnight the bells ring out
and from several quarters of the city, fireworks
flower. I try to see
not flak, not flares or tracers, but bougainvillea,
bougainvillea, bougainvillea. I try to think
how love is born tonight.

Back on the sidewalk, imploring Travelers
and The Hartford, I hold my paper cup close and
credulous as a child, consider speaking to the small
flame within, hoping to be in touch with someone
at the other end: *Ora pro nobis, ora pro nobis,*
ora pro nobis.

OUTSIDE IN

after the election, for Lonnie and Abu at Real Art Ways

Go home, the world says to the homeless huddled on rafts,
says *No* with ballots & guns. Today, a Red-bellied
is hammering a hole in clapboard by my window. *Come in,*

come in! that drumming says to red squirrels.
Bad bird! But something in me agrees, loves a wall
being undone in Berlin, in any home town, any heart.

I go back to last night's huddle of poets celebrating the life
of our friend, undoing the wall between us and
him, that new Outsider. We take in his homeless ghost.

For him Abu drums, hands blurring on taut goatskin,
palms, knuckles, fingertips, callused hand-heels drumming
an opening spacious enough for the dead, for all of us.

Come in, come in!

Abu goes on drumming, drumming-in whoever's out,
all things wanting habitat, all creatures endangered,
the wounded walking bomb-blasted refugee roads,

a Child freezing in December, last speaker of a tribal tongue.
Come in, come in. He is drumming us, outsiders, in
to the wide savannah of the past we share with him.

II. IN WILDERNESS

CHILD OF WAR

They are fleeing,
they are fleeing,
they are fleeing
the stench of war,
the empty space
where their homes
once stood.

They are fleeing
with empty hearts
in boats too small
for the sea
of grief.

They are drowning,
they are drowning.

Here is one
come ashore at
the edge of the surf.

He is three,
he is tucked in,
knees folded,
hands together,
afloat in the womb.

He will not wake.
He is at peace,
the only peace
the world
seems to know
how to make.

THE RETURNING

After sending them out, the Lord God stationed mighty
cherubim to the east of the Garden of Eden. And he placed
a flaming sword that flashed to and fro to guard the way
to the tree of life.   Genesis 3:24

Past thrust and parry of Antrim traffic, trust
a rope bridge to reach a currach to carry you
to Rathlin Isle. Pitch your tent
by the tallest oak, beacon for homing coot
at the knob of the island's elbow.
Like the first couple, find proper names for
a red scurry to the underbrush, a low umber
harry of finger-tipped wings . . .

Breathe, rest easy, let the gloaming deepen,
walk up an outstretched limb of the tree
sloping down to earth as if to lift you higher,
reach a crow's nest. Scan the strait, consider
the water road's ripple-rungs of moonlight,
how you might stride from one to the other
to the Mull of Kintyre, that next world so near
you're almost there, no fig leaves about you.

A BRIEF HISTORY
OF THE SKUNK CABBAGE

To find a heaven in a wild flower. —William Blake

It comes up in time to cure winter's ills.
Grind and boil shavings of its thick root stock,
chant the proper Chippewa Song of Healing,
imbibe, and begone your deep-rooted cough.

A salve from it will heal the fungus of your feet
and though it's toxic to things that uproot it
you can rub eight seeds of its brain-shaped fruit
on a bride's maidenhead for conception.

From its foot-thick, heavy-furred root stock
small spears of next year's version
and the one after that are already growing
in the muck it loves. Right now, this March,

look closely at the south-facing slopes
of any iced-in creek and see, in earth-brown
rings of leaf mold where it has melted snow,
the Skunk Cabbage

already up. It heats everything around it,
those blood-purple, gold-spotted spiral spathes
cracking winter's shell . . .
No, don't try to tie it down with metaphors —

it is simply itself, fetid yes, but sweet, sweet
to the carnal beetles and flies of March

seduced by so much delicious decay
it emulates in its birthing place,

that slit-doored shadowy recess
where the globe of a skin-beige blossom,
fleshy, all stamen and style, reclines, its parts
so much warmer than the winter beyond

its patrons revel, their fur riffled
by a warm breeze from the play of its heat
on the cold, as if fanned by a harem-master
in this pleasure dome.

ROOFING

One of the roofing crew has dropped his stack of shingles,
says "Come quick!" What accident, what hole in the roof,
I wonder, stumbling after him. Thick-necked and grizzled,
he leads me quickly to the scene. "I saw it from the ladder,
something prehysterical." And there, next to a small pit

that cradles a dozen beige, leathery eggs, a two-foot Snapper
carelessly flicks a mound of dirt with one rear leg, distracted
by our looming and the flash of the roofer's phone cam.
She loses heart, lumbers off, and the foreman reprimands
his workman, who returns to roofing, waves from a ladder.

That evening I go back to finish the job, discover
it's done. The dirt is level, a quick thatch of sticks and duff
over it, maybe enough to fool a coon or sharp-nosed skunk.
If the eggs are not stowed in the hope chest of a turtle brain
they're safe in the knob at the top of a roofers's spine.

AT THE PEBBLE BEACH PRO-AM

In the sky over such well-paid
combat presented by CBS –
players whaling away at Top-Flites
plus periodic assaults by IBM
and German engineering –
Snoopy II,

blunt-nosed, big-bellied defender
against the *if* in life, zeros in on

its distant cousins cruising Spanish Bay,
as clearly visible in their element
as Planet Earth afloat in the firmament
seen by loping moonmen planting a flag:

Gray Whale mothers paired with calves
on their way from birthing grounds
off Baja. They will travel 10,000 miles to
feast on arctic plankton. Border-hopping,
playfully all business, they have no time
for our endangered species.

LATE HEAVY BOMBARDMENT

*Recently, in geological terms – about 4 to 3.8 billion years
ago – a "Late Heavy Bombardment" of asteroids rich in
amino acids is said to have deposited the building-blocks of life.*

Beyond the book-size pane through which I see
the world, a Ruby Throat hovers, then dives to feast

on nectar invented back when. By what?
Or Whom? I'm wondering still, not having grown up.

Given the *Late Heavy Bombardment* of Earth in its middle
age, only four billion years ago – inexplicable comets

raining down at 25,000 mph, blasting craters
the size of Delaware, grab bags filled with tinker

toys for Evolution to play with, one small amino wheel
connected with a rod to another and another until

a paramecium is an orchid is a fish is is a kangaroo-
mouse is a hippopotamus – given all that,

I side with Creation: in the life of every body,
even late, there may be godly bombardments

enough to cause what was *formless and void* to birth
nectar and humming birds and verse.

RUBY THROATS IN SEPTEMBER

Biologists are uncertain why many species repeat
mating rituals late in the year.

Nights are longer, cooler, more enticing,
days brighter, crisper, more fruitful,
the instinct to travel building to a peak,
the nuzzling of nectar longer, more
exciting, the need to dance coming on
where they meet above the fuchsia,
a blossoming themselves – this standing
on air, this facing one another, coming
forward, moving back, all but touching
breasts, then dos-i-do-ing,
rising in spirals, back flips, barrel rolls,
loopings of the loop, one last fling
before the great migration to come
when they will dance from state
to state, arriving different and complete.

AUBADE BENEATH STEEP HILL

Like the strings of a harp, slender birches and oaks
on the slope of Steep Hill are played by last light
of the moon sliding in and out among them,
slim fingers of moon light and now a wider glow
like a harpist's palm on her strings. Hush, hush . . .

until the russet water music of a wood thrush calls
up the dawning mauve, violet, and rose
blush of western cumulus. And a second thrush
responds with the liquid anapest of *I am here*
in answer to the other's *Are you there?*

As the west continues to brighten in light of the east,
the antiphony quickens. *Are you there?*
I am here.
Are you there?
I am here.

THE WHITE ROSES OF LISSADELL

ancestral Irish home of the Gore-Booths

It was dark when we arrived late in the century
at the empty mansion, its sad doves singing vespers,
gone the song and dance of rebellious revelry
and Yeats, come to call with the burr of his poetry.

Like the lowered lids of all their eyes, the shades
were drawn. The old stone of Lissadell was the gray

of the deepening dusk, but there — uncultivated,
sharp-thorned, thick-stemmed, barbarously graceful

white roses. They once bedecked familial beauties,
the Gore-Booth girls, white-gowned in the evening
for a poet's visit, tall colleens dancing ghostly —
white roses celebrating the innocence of ceremony

from which we take cuttings,
hoping.

NEWS

It is difficult to get the news from poems, yet men die
miserably every day for lack of what is found there.
> —William Carlos Williams

Here's news for lack of which you'll live
more miserably: this hirsute bear of a man

is down on his knees and hands in the basement
where he's been growing a Floralina Tomato bush
all winter, coddling and sunning it every day.

He has his vibrator out, the electric toothbrush
he no longer bumbles over his mossy teeth.

He is placing its bristles behind each yellow flower,
buzzing anthers to rouse the fine-furred pollen
he blows upon. He is singing softly.

FIRE

Our newest glass partitions are both translucent and reflective,
creating optical illusions your customers will love.

         —Wholesale Catalogue, Allmerica Glass

Happily, during a reading at Polytech by
a poet celebrating Solstice, I managed to forget
that the fire behind him was purely gas.

Then the signing, sad dénouement. But beyond
a batch of made-up coeds milling about, the fire
turned a reflecting glass partition to nothing
but Looking Glass, breaking through like Alice

straight to the heart of the library proper where,
from banks of Macs, rows of technical journals,
the blue hair of a reference librarian
and the shoulders of several aspiring engineers,

flames burst like something out of William Blake!
The Poetry Fire was out there giving it a go.
Illusion, illusion —
I would not have it otherwise.

               for Jeff Harrison

AFTER THE READING

for Katharine Carle at 85

She'd said it all in song after song
at the podium. Then the fall, EMTs,
ER, after which the flesh fell away
on the screen where a Bone Doctor
showed the broken neck of the femur
just below its ball and socket fitting.
The Day of Judgment was now —
hip bone connected to the leg bone
no longer. There'd be no shaking
this. She waved goodbye, blew a kiss.
They put her under, then two days
of being neither awake nor asleep
while titanium married itself to bone.
On the third day she was herself
and the Heart Doctor looked into her
to see if her heart was to blame
and there — oh second miracle —
the baubles of her heart were going on
like belly dancers. How they sang and
sang their salty song!

WHILE THE WORLD AT LARGE GOES ALL TO HELL

the ruffed grouse dives into new-fallen snow
and propels itself like a porpoise
to tunnel to a place it wing-beats into a den
far enough in to fool a fox
and deep enough down to survive a freeze
and firmly floored enough to push off
if worldly danger comes too close, exploding
up and out like the first stage of a spacecraft
heading for a less polluted place.

And my ruffed grandson goes the grouse
one better—after a two-foot snowfall
he shovels and shovels, builds an 8-foot snowpile,
breaks out his army surplus "trenching tool,"
tunnels into the pile, carves out a den, builds
a small bonfire at its entrance,
invites his girlfriend over, burrows in with her...

Afterwards, they take charred sticks from the fire
and inscribe feral shapes on the walls of their cave,
a pig with wings, a crow on skis...
The ice wall steams as they work their creatures
into it with fire sticks. No woolly mammoths these
but they will do. The two explode with laughter,
seeing how well the world starts out all over again.

LOST ART

for the Charcoal Makers

They lived in the woods,
spoke Animal, built pyres
of oak, mounded them
with sod, ignited the cores,

tended the burns religiously,
bored holes for air
or filled them in to smother
the fire, slept in snatches,

revised, revised, tamping
the surface matter above
the oak turning to charcoal
in a lethal truth of fire

into which at times they fell,
were lost to us, consumed.
But they gave us something
better than a later century's

soft and crumbling briquets –
gave us uncompromising
nuggets hard, clean, essential
to hearth and heart.

May such an art not be lost
on those who should adjust
their fire, revise and revise
otherwise.

III. SERENADES

PABLO'S CELLO

I love the way he attends to every part
of me beforehand —
rubs my *neck* and *shoulders,* runs his hand
down the narrows of my *waist,*
deftly adjusts my heart-shaped tuning pegs.

And now the tremolo of his touch
on my fingerboard, the slow and faster,
short or longer, light or firmer touch of bow
sliding from one to another of my strings,
his handbeat on my *hip* for good measure.

I thrill with vibration he sends through me,
magnify it in the legs he wraps me with
and lips that all but touch my lowest string.

HOLDING ON

for my Chevy S-10

She doesn't stop and start the way she used to;
there have been issues with her fluids;
her pressure is erratic — too high, too low;
her bushings are worn, her bottom tender
where time has been at it . . .

She's a bit bionic in her parts, but all the better
for it. I'm holding on to her for our dear life.
My God, they don't make 'em that way any more.

SERENADE

I sing the gibbous moon's waxing,
its polishing things seen darkly,
turning them milk-blue;
sing the surge
of the sea toward what was torn away,
left a gap in our pacific world;
sing the lunar urge of salt-blood to swell
the shriveled husks of us;
sing the terrible need of separated things
for one another.

THAT FIRST NIGHT

couldn't last, I knew, though it did
and did, but by morning was simply
memory. I'm reminded
how the men of Xi'an digging a well,
striking one of 8000 terra cotta figures,
brilliant red, blue, gold, jade preserved
beneath a lacquer sheen,
must have gasped at such extravagant
luxury; and how in the ordinary air
the paint flaked off with the lacquer,
was dust, until barely four minutes later
the figure was merely khaki clay.
But the men of Xi'an had seen, and they
were guided by wonder all their days.
Just so, that first time is with me always,
love. Each of my eight thousand days
is illuminated by the night. My clay
bears the brilliant sheen of immortality.

RECOMPOSITION

for Clara Schumann and Johannes Brahms

Telling his story, Brahms' *Quartet for Piano & Strings*
in its C minor yearning and anguish rises into notes
of such clarity and beauty in G major that this serenade
from Johannes to Clara is more than the *Sorrows*
of Young Werther for which the piece is named.
Perhaps their love need not end, as the minor key says
it must, in disrepair and parting.

We know the story: how her husband fell
apart despite all Clara could do, threw his ring and
then himself into the Rhine, ended in a madhouse,
jealous of her fame and genius;
how Johannes came to stay, boarded in an upper story
of the Schumann home, consoled Clara,
helped with the children and chores, sharing
the memory of Robert, whose music both adored;
and how when he died, the pair fled to Switzerland
to marry; and how it all fell apart as surely as Robert.

It is uncomfortable to see them at the inn in Gersau.
Her need for him is unreserved. She has removed
all she wore, but he just his shoes and waistcoat.
When she opens to him, he turns away.

Try to understand. Follow him
to where, a young 15, he played an upright
for his living at a bistro by the sea, enchanted
by the girls who made a living upstairs. He was lost
in a tumult of love for the youngest of them

until one afternoon he found her
with legs wrapped around a burly sailor just in
from the North Sea fleet,
her cry of delight the very one reserved for him.

Now in Gersau Clara pulls him to her on the bed,
undresses him, forgets the world,
cinches him with thighs, calves, digs in her heels,
makes a sound so feral he pushes her away,
will not say a word. She hides her face.

Next day, a curt farewell, he resorting to his career,
she to hers, feeling "as if returning from a funeral."

Here in the Music Shed the Piano Quartet is in full
career with the anguish of all that C Minor
denied at times by such sublimity in G Major
we see, with Brahms, the scene reversing:

Clara's cry funnels into her throat, her legs relent.
She remembers the story of the sailor, runs a hand
through the hair of her Johannes, gentles him,
draws back far enough for him
to see clearly the full face of her love.
His face unclenches . . .

The history of music will be different.
They will marry, he will encourage her
to compose the music that threatened Robert,
the music Johannes yearns to hear.
The world will be richer.

REMBRANDT ROOM

after Rembrandt van Rijn's studies of Hendrickje
Stoffels and his last self-portrait of 1669 – all
in Room 23 of the National Gallery in London

Short of beautiful, she is substantial,
his common law wife
the church calls concubine. Now
she returns to the chiaroscuroed bed
for his "Portrait of Hendrickje Stoffels,"
having just rinsed off the juice of love.

Happily naked, she covers herself to
entice him, dons two of his treasures –
a gold bead necklace draped low
to underscore her generosities of breast
and a careless ermine stole revealing
the edge of a rubicund nipple. She looks
straight at us, her face still flushed,
her large black eyes deep pools of dare
as if to say "So?"

She fondles a ruddy cone-shaped knob
on the post of the bed
she has no intention of leaving, not even
here, hung on a side wall at the National.

Hendrickje means to please him all ways,
no matter his age – it is, she says,
the Age of Rembrandt. She plans to be
part of his age. No younger man will do.
She sells his work, grinds his paint.

For his part, he stretches
canvas for her portrait of Cornelia,
the daughter they desired, the work
they have wrought.

Where he poses her is always where
she wants to be, like the cooling stream
he has found for her. Stepping in,
Hendrickje hikes up her skin-beige shift
to the dark fur at the crux of her.
Delighting in the moment, her mouth
not yet wholly smiling but inclining
that way, she slides her left foot into
the stream by the entry to Room 23.

Knobby knees, broad sloping shoulders,
unkempt hair — the unruliness of her
is a pleasure to Rembrandt, raising
his impasto knife to work gold
into the hem she is lifting higher now.
During a break, she tosses the shift.
Come swim with me, her full smile says.

Hung on the far wall, looking her way,
his last self-portrait is roughed out,
undone —
blotched face furrowed, eyes grieving
for the death by Plague of Hendrickje.

There at the easel, stalled,
facing the mirror image of his despair,
he must but cannot define the end
of who he is, and unwilling to see it,

she leans toward him from
her somber portrait in velvet beret
on loan from the Louvre . . .

But it's their daughter who appears
in the mirror to one side of his canvas,
fresh from slicing lemons for sole,
and runs a cool hand across his brow
and through the tangles of his hair
as his love so often did, pleasing him
in this and every way. She looks

so much like her mother
he knows Hendrickje will continue,
heart wild as a trout in the stream
she enters with him.

Cornelia, the daughter of Rembrandt and Hendrickje,
bore two children named Rembrandt and Hendric.

ASCENDING AT THE NEUE

after Egon Schiele's "Man and Woman" (1914)
and Marianne Von Werefkin's "Prayer" (1910)

At the Gallery, a pair of lovers are flagrantly naked.
He is dark, angular, with enormous arms and hands
extended like pincers, lying on his back
surrounded by a mountain of bedsheets hurled off,

beside a woman on her knees and elbows, hind quarters
raised, cleft like a heart. Head lowered, she looks
back between her legs to see him come behind her,
her head all but lost. He stares point blank at me.

I have no business here,
am pleased my heavy feet work
well enough to reach the upper level of the show,
bent as I am and holding tight to the curving banister.

I am suddenly face to face with a place I believe in.
Here, night comes on at a blue country shrine.
Framed in its niche, a naked man,
crossed, hands and feet nailed, has had the breath
taken from him.
The man's head hangs limply, his white loin cloth
scant protection. Bent-backed before him

is another man, the white jut of his beard
matching the white of the first man's final apparel
and the snow-dazzled peaks
beyond the rough landscape he has come through,
which now, in the gloaming, shines with all
the greens and golds, lavenders and reds of late day.

Above, a crescent moon begins. Rings of blue sound
radiate from it as if from the bell of the shrine
still resonating.

The bent man says nothing to the Christ, nothing
I hear aloud, until I don his dark pilgrim coat, pray,
drop the coat to the ground, naked before the truth.
I hold nothing back, am fully at peace, more in love
than the lovers a level below will be for many years.

HANDS

Descending from the second story,
I steady myself, hand sliding on the handrail,
then polishing the knob of the newel.

Time has worn away its gray, revealing
the rose of earlier days and hints of darker
shades below. For over two hundred years
and twelve wars, such a scoring by hands.

In the wash of history, time shrinks.
I remember placing my palm on the red ochre
print of a hand in a Utah cave, surprised
by the almost perfect fit.

At the newel, I fit my hand to the backs of
other hands that touched its round in passing:
hands of lovers ascending,
hands of mourners descending, slow hands
of the old, quick of the children rushing by.

And I feel the hands of those to come,
the sad and the joyful taking their turns,
their palms brushing the back of my hand
where it rests on the newel.

Selections from

VISITATIONS

SONG OF OVID

You, Caesar,
exile me to the end
of the world and

I'll not cease
to dip my quill
in the dark well

of wine dregs,
soot and
black squid jet

to fashion
the clarity of
song.

I. A DELICACY OF BEASTS

ARCHIBALD & THE STARLING

He's sick of it.
His id is dead, dreams dry.
Yesterday he found himself laid out,
chalk white on the black

board. Some student had done him
(egg head, clown tufts, big goggles)
perfectly. Cruel, cruel.
Ah well, it's April. He's doing Eliot

with them — *Here we go round*
the prickly pear prickly pear prickly
too early in the morning.
At dawn today he'd rather decipher

a star-spangled starling in the old maple,
hollow, ant-ridden, cabled together.
So what if the tree sprouts
Jerusalem artichokes

from its rot, reminds him of the fur
in his ears. What's that
to the starling? The bird seems to think
a tree this far gone

is the best
platform for what's to mimic —

blare of a horn, catch of an engine,
cry of a lover, such morning music

that Archibald rehearses his own
en route to Am Lit. He climbs
into his head, praises its defoliation,
cancels class, composes this.

GOING ON

The American Elm is defunct. None
arch like ceremonial swords above
East Avenue or fountain like tall vases

flowering. But today, still winter,
I find a small rusty thing with wings
fallen from a stunted half-dead elm

to roadside mud, already half open
for a seed with plans.
So much, extinct, goes on and on.

GOOD FRIDAY

"The woodcock, in essence, has an upside-down brain."
            — NY Dept. of Environmental Conservation

It's that rare Good Friday when the moon's come full
circle, as utter as I've ever seen it, and the night
warm enough for wood frogs and humming toads
with the Dog Star strobing green, blue, red, yellow,
and Venus low in the west
huger than usual, Jupiter not bad either, just below her.

Here I am, between a bog and a moon-blue field,
wanting you with me to say what I hear is what I hear:
something in the alders like a cut-off kazoo's *beeent, beeent,*
then the whirring wing-warble of a bird's quick take-off,
the moon-struck shine of its sky-circling high
in the constellated night, and round on round of chirruping
before the woodcock spirals wildly down, a whistle of wings

to ground—then more *beeeeeent beeeeeeent beeeeeeeent . . .*
Like the bird's, my brain's upside down from staring up so long.
If such sounds come to me in my problematic state
with no one else to hear, does this bird-thou-never-wertness
exist at all? Or I? In theory I know what *it* is, who *I* am,
but doubt my theory. Now a stirring in the alders near the place
he landed. She was watching, apparently approves, wants more,

for he clacks his double-jointed beak like a circus seal clapping
and repeats the show. He is, therefore I am?
We'll see. We're in this together, the woodcock, you and I.
Beeeeeent beeeeeeent. RSVP.

BECAUSE EASTER

always comes after the first full moon
of spring, I'm thinking
of putting the Easter Moon into a poem,

something about "the new moon grown
ripe as a wood frog's song-full throat."
Good God, that's awful!

Happily I'm interrupted – you bring me
an orange button dug up in the garden,
the shell of a newborn painted turtle,

dime-size. It must have hatched during
our cold spell from an egg wintered over,
perfect little legs, tail, head . . . but defunct.

We commiserate, and I put the button in
the waste basket among wadded up
copies of my poem

and go on revising. It's hopeless. I give up,
am returning to figures on a spreadsheet
when I hear a spondaic scratching among

the waste of words. I dig out the Painted,
its legs busily making for water. The thrust
of its neck is easterly.

BACK UPS

Woooooooooah woooaaaaaaaah
they sing, *wooooooooooooooooooooah*
sing the Common American Toads

behind a serenade of courting frogs
like backups for Sha Na Na
or Bobby Vee

all the songful night.
But they don't go steady –

some chime in while others
chime out – to go at the thing
the chiming's all about.

DELICACY

Out of hiding,
grown fat on berries, lilies, and all manner
of lush refuse, shambled the dream bear –
and does so more and more this morning,

now that I'm telling you how he appeared
under the almost full moon at 10 last night
to delicately bend the feeder pole just enough
to fell the seed, how he laid all 500 pounds

down and like a child spooning ice cream
from a Dixie cup, slowly – to make it last –

raised careful paw-scoops of sunflower seed
to his mouth and closed his eyes

to savor completely the incredible
oils of seed, each in its small way sleek and fat
as the bear who grew increasingly actual
with a yellow tag in his ear to which he paid

no more mind than he did to the floodlight
exposing him. But he's paying close attention
as I repair the feeder now, fill it for birds –
no, him. He watches from the deep

of the woods out back, waiting – while I
prepare the way for such bestial delicacy.

GARDEN

It might be snakes coupling, this counter
clockwise writhe in the broccoli patch.
I approach warily.

There are six or seven, like small rats,
but browner, in an ecstasy of hunger,
ears almost transparent
with the sun shining through, a white spot
on each forehead like a miner's lamp,

behind which small brains are beginning
to consider the garden an Eden
for rabbits.

When I pick one up, its fur is so slicked
I see how new to this they are.

Thinking of squash blossoms
and leaves of arugula
demolished,
I will this part of the plot to them.

AUBADE

At 5 a.m. an alarming nuthatch
with a case of avian dementia
repeats and repeats a monotone

Get up get up   Get up get up
Get up . . . But now this liquidity
of a thrush more deeply in the wild

commending sloth, his song
ascending and descending languidly,
eases me like the vision Jacob had

on the lam, his head pillowed
on desert stone — a visitation of
leisurely angels on their ladder

in pre-dawn's lavender light,
their slow dance suggesting the way
to be, out of joint from all-night

wrestling with an angel: *Sleep in*
today. Amen, I say, cheek to cheek
with rumpled sheets.

ROMANCE OF THE ROSE-BREASTED GROSBEAK

If you think love's not blind
just listen to him singing his elaborate love song
as she takes her pleasure at the feeder she's emptying,
selecting only the choicest sunflower seed.

Dandy in a black and white zoot suit the morning after,
he wears his bleeding heart on his chest
(see how the point of it drips). And the object of all his
colorful affection

is this scrawny, big-beaked, dun-colored little dinosaur
tossing seed over her shoulder. Her only bright spot
is a pair of white stripes swept back from her beady eyes
like the sidebars of the godawful spectacles
on some mousy secretary.

Still, the way her handsome boyfriend is ogling her
gives me pause. Who's blind here? God knows,
when she takes off those glasses, lets down her hair . . .

THE TAO OF MILKWEED

"It is more blessèd to be ministered unto
than to minister," says Asclepias
the Milkweed, unabashedly amoral.

"If it were not my ministry to be delighted
by all who thrive on me, I'd never have
devised the several ways I service them:

the honey-hiving Sybarites who frequent
the lubricious boudoirs of my blossoms,
transporting me with lengthening tongues;

inchworms hunched as omegas stretching
to tickle the fur of my leaves, turning
nicely toxic with my concoction;

witches and warlocks curing their warts
with the milk I secrete for them, in love
as any suckling mother with expressing;

the fall wind that dandles and undoes me,
absconding with the fine silk tassels
of peacock-eyed seed-chutes I release

to the will of the wind
making much of me in the field it fills
with more and more of what I am."

STAYING ALIVE

I too dislike the rasping, redundant repetition
of the Tufted Titmouse
but this —
its mortal mandala at the base of the feeder

where the Sharp-shin hit home: a spray of down
and lesser feathers, and arranged centrifugally,
primaries plucked off one by one from
the dumb throbbing thing before its ascension.

Now chickadees, cardinals, finches come
and go at the feeder as if they don't – but they
do – know what's up. What courage it takes
to stay alive.

SQUIRRELS

Squirrels can flick the bushy brag of their tails all they want;
they are still rats. Grey, red, and black rats. They think
the birdseed belongs to them. But they do have their ways:

go high-wiring along the clothesline holding the feeder,
and better, after some contemplation, bite the line in half,
bring down the seed.

All right, let's raise the bar. I set the feeder on a pole
I grease and baffle, wait for them to weasel up, and think
of you, mother – how while you were waiting to die

you kept an eye on your seed, watched the squirrels sway
the lilac next to it for momentum, then leap to the feeder.
How you laughed, preparing for your own crossing over.

VISITATION

I've been anxious all morning,
have come outside to sit by the fall flowers,
shaggy orange and pink and yellow zinnias
grown tall for the occasion

beside the rough-hewn slats of a barn-red barn.
The day is warming after a touch of frost.
The zinnias have made it through

and have a caller
on orange-red, black-veined wings
rimmed with white dots and yellow oblongs.
The wings go from flower head to
head, landing, shutting, opening slowly,
then folding together like supplicant hands
palm to palm for the long deep drawing in,
and rising for delighted swags of dizzy flight
up and down the length of the barn
before lighting on another zinnia.

Perhaps this Monarch has no bad dreams,
perhaps every shag of zinnia,
every beam of light and shade, every slice of sky
is a close relation, every zig sensational,
rehearsal for riding to a height
from which to glide to the next updraft,
all the way to some valley in Mexico ingrained
in a Monarch's half gram of memory.

I drink it all in, so much late-life delight, this
storing up for the long trip to come.

II. REFUSAL TO MOURN

POSTPARTUM

is pretty much everywhere. It strikes
lovers after love, epicures after feasting,
babes in arms forever after coming out
and poets after readings –

all suffer postpartum
and pine for what they had before
or wish it had been more.

Which explains
why we have more babes
than we can handle, and Rocky 2,

also my newest work you're hearing here.
I revel in its figment of completion
but no . . . already I'm growing postpartum
until the next consummation

of a verse or – god help us – publication,
that detonation of rose petal drifting
into a canyon . . . inducng more postpartum.

INTERVALS

I'm listening to Miles play
"So What," all that gorgeous
silence between measures
for us to fill in

like the space Lady D made

in the blues
for riffs by Lester, slow
eyes on him.

When Lester died, then Lady,
so much empty space
stopped Sonny from playing
Birdland (the Bird gone too).

He was silent all day
and wailed all night, out there
on the Williamsburg Bridge,
alone. For weeks. Every night.

When he came in
late, he'd telephone Trane,
wail a phrase,
subside,

create the necessary interval
for pain to fill, releasing
that perfect tenor sax of Trane's,
They never spoke.

OFF HOUR OF THE SAINTS

after "Meeting of St. Anthony and St. Paul" by Pietro Sassetta

See how these saints-to-be lurch at each other,
canes tossed aside: two old men not acting their age.
They're spent from wrestling demons in the desert.
Even saints must yearn for furlough.

One of Anthony's bare feet strokes Paul's instep
and the hands of each are on the other's buttocks.
below the chocolate trunks and candied boughs
of the fig trees shading this oasis and its cave.

The saints are so cheek to cheek their heads
are all but one, a keystone to their bodies' arch.
Their lavishly Byzantine halos clang, will be hung
like weapons by the cave's dark mouth.

BERNINI'S ANGEL

I prefer Bernini's clay mockups
(thumbprints still lively on their skin)
to his finished marbles and bronzes

like the angels he covered with drapery
and posed along the Ponte Sant'Angelo
for the Pope to bless.

I prefer his angels in their native state
composed of earthy stuff
like this muscular one in the raw,

legs and torso torqued as if to hurl
his discus, though it is in fact the Crown
of Thorns he has in hand,

wild from Calvary. And such wings!
Not the wings of heavenly choir boys
or the melting pasted-ons of Icarus,

but wings that surged like a raptor's
a moment ago beneath the Cross
from the blades of his furious shoulders.

ON GIVING A GIFT OF MILKWEED

In World War Two, milkweed provided the kapok
used in Mae West life preservers.

I bring no flowers for him in hospice
but a bird-like pod, its soft inner lip
dividing twin seed-rooms, its curling,
life-saving seed-silk lapping
the edges, dark eyes looking to fly.

I remember collecting such pods
for the boys at the Front in '43, unsure
precisely how the silk would save
their lives, but oh, wanting them
saved, and scooping the milkweed,
fistfuls of it, into my burlap.

Half a century later I know — from the way
a dying man runs his finger over
the satin lining of this small seed house
and with his slight of breath
sets its cargo adrift in the room —
how it might bring a soul at sea
safely into harbor.

A LIVING

O dark dark dark. They all go into the dark.
  —T.S. Eliot, "East Coker" (*Four Quartets*)

[handwritten: Everything goes into]
They all go into the dark,
even their names.
[handwritten: Arns in water]
I hold my arms before me, dowsing,
feel a stirring in my fingertips, am
drawn by love to the underworld,

and think of the beautiful manatees *[handwritten: Half human]*
[handwritten: my stical]
hides inscribed, cabalistic, rising *[handwritten: rebirth]*
in the warmth of Homosassa River
[handwritten: Florida]
[handwritten: human to underworld]
far enough to ask me in
to revel in nameless devolution

to web feet, and from there
to gills, simplification to a group
of similar-minded cells,
a flagellant, then the loveliness
of nothing at all, that siren call *[handwritten: Odyseus]*

[handwritten: suicidal?]
I'm tempted by, and deny. I will stay
[handwritten: boat = life]
on board, relish my name,
the craft of my life, ride it crowning *[handwritten: Birth]*
through narrow straits to the arms of
a harbor, a love expecting me, a living.
[handwritten: wife / himself]

[handwritten: Journey of life]

[handwritten: dark / Death: Below water]
[handwritten: light / Life: Above water]

SONG FOR DECEMBER FIRST

How the spirit can go dark,
long for a curling burrow
and still not go to ground.

I learn from possums the art
of weathering winter,
am in love

with the way a body can go on
despite how little it feels
its whereabouts, despite the bent

of a collapsing spine,
despite the absence of blood
from its usual haunts.

I listen to it carve its channels
below the freeze of hand and foot.
Oh give me this day this very day.

NAMING

Blessèd those who believe like Adam that to name a thing
is to make it real, like directing pure Energy (mc^2)
into the thick of Higgs Field (that runaway truck ramp)
to slow it, get a handle on it, make it matter.

Blessèd are the believers who chant the names of God —
Adonai, Yahweh, El, Allah, Jehovah, I Am That I Am . . .
(101 names says Meher Baba) an abacus of names to bring
God into being. The more our belief, the more His names.

Blessèd to believe the names (the Persians counted 1000)
like *pi* go on increasing in one enormous wave.
Blessèd those for whom to speak even one of the names
of God is to bring all the others into play.

And blessèd the lovers, saints-in-training, who name
each other with numberless names, a new one each day,
the increase a sign of their degree of adoration.
Like Plato's revelers they climb the Rungs of Love.

SOLSTICE CELEBRATION AT
THE RETIREMENT COMMUNITY

*The end of the world was to occur, according
to ancient predictions, on December 21, 2012.*

The day before the end of the world
we gathered around a bonfire, sparks
rising to the wind-rocked crescent moon
one of us called the Advent Cradle.

We beat pots and pans, blew whistles

to encourage what gave light to the moon.
One Druid in our circle muffed her hand
in the puppet she'd made for the occasion,
raised and lowered its stripling arms
beating a toy drum she held for it to play.

We read "Stopping by Woods" in unison:
The woods are lovely dark and deep
but I have promises to keep
and miles to go before I sleep
and miles to go before I sleep.

We made resolutions
to keep our promises – there'd be a Child
in the cradle and how many others needing
our attention before we trekked into
the deep and lovely dark.

ITO-SAN AND THE TSUNAMI

Noriko Ito-san had just put on her white
split-toe geisha socks

and was starting to elaborate her hair
for the night's entertainment at the ryōtei

when the ground shook, the walls cracked,
and twelve minutes later the ocean struck.

At 82, the oldest geisha in Ryoishi-cho,

she'd been through this before. Four times.

But now, with her asthma and bad knees,
there was no escaping

the sea tearing down the city, the sirens
shrill, deafening her one good ear.

With which, Mizuko Marukī, a spry 59,
bent low before Ito-san,

took her on his back and ran toward
a nearby hill as the surge, 20 feet high

behind him, swept cars and all before it.
Later he reported, "She is the only one

knows all the old songs of Ryoishi,
and Ito-san sang the one she had prepared

for that evening, the one to encourage
a young Samurai going into his first battle.

She's small, a fine-boned beauty still,
though surprisingly substantial.

Her performance put strength in my legs
and others around us. We all survived."

In the hospital where Ito-san recovered
her breath, she raised her voice to sing

"The Ryoishi Seashore Song" in praise,
she said, of the Greater Wave.

SEA AND SHORE SONG

In the main they are entirely engaged.
She swells, crests, rides up his strand
with a whisper of foam, turns
his continent stone to bright sand

so fine he flows like sea,
she thickens like land.
His straight edge curls to bays, crescents
of playground where she toys with him.

But there are times
when they rage against each other.
She rises up, arches her neck, strikes
the hex-eyed fishing boats on his beach,

surges into his dwellings, drowns all.
And he hurls fire at the sky. Runnels of it
flow down his heights, ignite the night,
boil into her, keep her steaming for days.

This is not what they wish. The urge for it
is beyond them,
takes them by surprise. When it subsides
at last, they are undone, exhausted.

And one night a ribbon of moon unspools
from her to him, wraps them in remembrance
of their days. Once again she swells, crests,
comes on him with a whisper of foam,

nestles in his coves, brings him bright sand

so fluid that where they meet he flows
like sea, she thickens like land.
She carries him in her.

STORMY WEATHER

for Katharine Carle

When the warning was issued — *Take cover:*
damaging winds and hail, possible tornado —
the old lady in 21-E prepared

by finding her sou'wester and
stepping out to her second-story porch
at the complex where she was

trouble. The blacker it got, the more she
brightened in the face of the fast-coming hits
of lightning turning her yellow slicker

gaudy as a tavern's nightly neon.
If it was her time, it was. In the meantime
she had one more opening on her card.

She lifted her arms in a V, spun about and
kicked up her legs, the old bones reveling,
pitched like a tuning fork to the clappings

of thunder so close now there was no time
to recite *Mississippi One* before a bolt struck
fifty yards from her and bowled its way

into the gutter, narrowly missing. And that

set her off, her dance a tarantella now.
Oh Lord, this hell was heaven.

And when it was over
and the flattened meadow out back steamed
in the sudden cool the storm had left in its wake,

she felt so consummated but also so in need of play
she picked up a fistful of hail stones
littering the porch and like any girl in love

with the boy next door, threw them at the picture
window just down from hers belonging to a pillar
of the church, retired, hoping to die in peace.

REPORT FROM STATEN ISLAND

9.11.2002

After the last red gleam of twilight
through the gaps
between the remaining towers of the City,
their lights rising up like fire ladders,

uncertain of our footing
on this sad height, leaning into a rising wind
and holding one another, two old protesters
facing another world

at war, we sadly watch the beautiful ships,
brave running lights shining, as they ply

the harbor or float down from above
to land as if such grace

could never end. Now from Battery Park,
fireworks – bright umbrellas in the sky
so inappropriate and necessary we sing a little
facetiously at first, *sotto voce,* then more

and more certainly the words of the Anthem
we have so long distrusted, strain hopelessly
for that impossibly high C, the tattered banner
of our voices whipped by wind.

REFUSAL TO MOURN

for Norah Pollard

From the hurtle of traffic where I-95 crosses the Housatonic
you can see the tower downriver – no flag up, no play today
or tomorrow or tomorrow. The Shakespeare Theater,
that latter day Globe, is defunct.

Vermin root like groundlings in the seats
where I once watched Prospero stage his tempest.
The "flies" from which a cave, a bog, and a beach descended
are full of bats. Scat's everywhere above and below. It stinks.

Outside, the sculpture is doing no better. Blackly brooding,
a heavy-handed Hamlet, posing as The Thinker, thinks.
The blanks of his eyes, which once gazed philosophically
at Hepburn's stilted sea-shack being razed,

are painted out and run like an amateur Gloucester's bleeding
down cheeks on which pink bubble gum's been pasted.
Nearby, a bust of our young 35th President has been beheaded
by hoodlums owning these grounds, leaving a trail of condoms,

and from JFK across the Sound, escaped from Mexican crates,
have come these unlikely lime-green, blue-winged parakeets
squawking and defecating where Renaissance minstrels once
strolled to entertain a lawnful of theater-goers.

This Spring is full of discontent. The parakeets are homeless,
didn't predict the tempests of a Connecticut winter
would topple their enormous nests, those fifty-pound
galaxies spun from woven sticks.

Complete with clever bottom entries and antechambers,
the nests litter the grounds of the theater, but their fall
has not been enough to keep the birds from starting again,
reconstructing their tree town this spring.

Now enter this other
still more theatrical item from farther off – huge blackbird
with the white neck bib and talk-talk-talk of a magpie
and an eye for any pretty thing he can steal, like the lady love

he has taken from some smaller, more traditional crow.
For her, applying what he has learned from the parakeets,
who've given up mobbing him, he's building atop the theater
a most uncrow-like crow's nest. Oh brave new world.

And this:
though the minstrels no longer stroll these grounds,
others do – in particular a sort of Miranda and her swain,
strange pair, she in her thrift shop feathers and glad rags,

he in ragged, fish-ripe jeans.
He has a record but has gone somewhat straight, surveyor
and recorder of all he sees from Bond's Dock just down shore,
where he hangs out in his van. Betimes she joins him there,

his Boswell, although she fights with him like any Kate and
goes off by herself to sit at the feet of Hamlet, where she thinks
how much she hates to think, then cozies up to Hamlet
and thinks of nothing

but collecting the rich brown-and-beige gems fallen
at Hamlet's feet from the only chestnut the town hasn't felled
on the grounds to make room for vandal-proof light poles.
She fills her pockets with chestnuts, then returns to the dock

where she and her van man watch the Housatonic muscling
into the Sound and the Sound muscling into the Housatonic.
In winter they watch the ice racking up on the ice, grinding
and grinding and shaking the piles of the dock.

Things shake her too – his booze, his bouts – but always
she returns to him. Now enter from the wings again
the big crow (he's an African Crow). Who knows what's in it
for him at the dock. Maybe he's drawn by the stench

of the fish the dockeys catch – or by the palaver he'd like to
master, the better to mock. But Jim (he's Miranda's van man)
is ahead of him, has learned quick as a crow to talk Crow,
which she, weaver of words that she is, fancies

as she fancies the way he pats his arm,
pats and pats it
until Oreo (that's his name) comes and sits on the arm
as if Jim's some sort of newfangled St. Francis.

Miranda (they call her Paddy) has no idea what he says to Oreo. It's the music of it she loves and loosely translates as the necessary bard. All of which is why, though there's plenty to mourn, they don't.

OUTAGE

for Norah Pollard

After the storm, you call
to say you heard an explosion
from the mini-mall,
then another,

and saw tongues of fire
running along the power line –
transformers blown as far
as Lordship and beyond,

all those computers and cash
registers etc. kaput,
delighting you,
never high on the digital age.

And what's that
sound in the background –
another parakeet? No, you say,
finches, baby finches

you found fallen from a tree
(such a storm, so much wind)
wrapping one another with

their wings,

not quite dead
yet, and brought inside,
relocated in a woolen ski hat.
And now the sound

grows louder. They like what
you feed them, damp cat kibble
from a tweezer. The cats
complain, get extra catnip.

The way you deal with outage
throws a breaker in my brain.

GOOD NEWS

The coyotes have been coming closer:
last night they yipped and howled
in the backyard.

The Arctic is melting and today,
as ever, the rain is laced with acid,
with black rain to come. Also,
a Great Horned has done in the cat.

It's not surprising a prophet arrives
and pulls out a *Lighthouse*
with its usual warning.

I have in mind what they say:
always welcome strangers who land
at your door — you never know.

Anyway she's pretty in her bare feet
and I've always been a sucker for
revelations. We talk so long

the sun has time to come out.
After she leaves, the storm begins
to re-accumulate, but there they are:

the wet-on-brick prints of her feet,
slim and fine and blessedly naked,
not yet vaporized.

FINDING THE MUSE

for Hugh Ogden

Barely making it up Parnassus in first,
in and out of potholes on switchbacks made
by creative types who failed engineering,
the Fiat fumes and sputters like the cabby
who could as easily have had a fare for Athens.

Even a single Muse will do, a minor one,
or general inspiration, at least a view.
We level out where busloads of the faithful
block the view with cameras clicking

like the taxi meter.

Happily I'm shown to a cave — ah, a castle
for Calliope and all her sisters
until my eyes grow large enough to see
a carpet of sheep shit blue with age
and spattered with the scat of bats. I opt

for a mountain bistro, retsina. And then —
where buses were, just sky. The clouds have
names like *Naxos, Skiros, Ithaka*.
Bounding down the mountain, goat feet
slapping stone

whap whap, lungs fortissimo enough
to make several of him, the cabby
waves the purple, yellow and azure weeds
he has picked for the vase
on the dashboard by his meter.
For a moment its rhythm is an inspiration.

ROUNDING THE BEND

October's the rasp of ten-inch catalpa leaves
landing at my feet where I'm running the dog.
He's all nose, examines the fading

scent of the neighbor's Lab on foundations
the Lab no longer waters. We're unprepared

for the zip of a 10-speeder rounding the bend

and disappearing down the road. No hands. Look,
the biker's holding his long arms straight out,
dipping them this way, that way, like any hawk,

and before he's gone for good, lifting them up
in a V. He holds it, holds it. I hold up my own.

CROOKED MAN, CROOKED MILE

A breath of fresh air does little
good tonight, the world being so
intent on self-destruction.

Passing the nature preserve, I hear
shots — someone jacklighting.
Now, turning the corner,

I see, angled ahead in the sky,
the handle of the Dipper
that's also the tail of Ursa the Bear.

It traces precisely the crook
in the crooked road leading to a dip
where the bobcats and whitetails

cross, and where the coin of a waxing
moon reflecting in Jessie's Creek

is the token I need
to cross a crooked stile to a world
whose people do not see eye-to-eye
with rifled steel

but bend it
to other purposes.

SUBWAY SCENE

The girl tapping a tapered white cane,
her harnessed bull terrier seeing
her home, descends to the IRT platform,
stares straight ahead, the dog nervous,
growling at first

at a small group gathering about her.
They talk to each other as people do not
in the numb remove of the underground

about a change in the weather —
the city rinsed, clouds scattering,
5th Avenue lit for Christmas last night.
I don't understand, but when she smiles
and lifts her head to the above, I see.

RESTORATION

for Robin, in the Czech Republic

Forging hipbooted through sodden waist-high wheat,
my baronial son forgets how crippled I am, following him
to the manor house I really must see, he says, must
approach from its best side.

"We'll earn our magic," he says, and without looking back
at the hobbler behind him,
plunges into a tangled mess of nettles, briars, downed limbs
and mossy rocks fit for an old man to break his coccyx on.

Now through a gap, there it is, the magic rough indeed —
a baroque beauty once, but broken down
beyond repair, the third story fallen to the first,

a manor let go
after Herr Commandant retreated in '45.
The end is quick when vermin and weather invade,
I think, but my son claims proper restoration is the trick,

then turns, looks at me. *Looks.* We trek home more slowly.
He breaks off gothic spires of purple lupine, three-foot
lengths of it he lays out on a stone wall, already wilting like
lopped bodies after some natural disaster. He cuts, places

the stalks in water, marshals them into a brave bouquet.
"Everything can be made right,"
he says, and puts the flowers in my room.

PASSAGE

Unshod, my carry-ons conveyed, x-rayed,
arms out as wings, I'm wanded, declared
ready for flight. Oh blessèd dispossession –

how much you, distant cousin, vanishing
aught behind the observation window,
are the object of a gravity I leave behind.

I rise above you through cloud cover
to a blue vault from which I look down on
the plane's shadow moving cursively . . .

Day darkening, I see, close in the window
beside me, my face is yours, dear cousin,
becoming our Grandfather's, his

my son's. I adjust my watch, feel the tug
of gravity, and in our long descent I know
the names the shadow was spelling out.

FAMILY SNAPSHOT

for J and M

In their mother's Kodak Brownie
two beautiful boys are framed.

At 12 the older, chin on knuckles,
is in a Rochester Red Wings uniform,
on one knee as if in the on-deck circle,

his warm-up swings done.
Next to him the younger at 4 is caught
in mid-surprise, having just been handed

the mitt in which he holds the hardball
caught by his brother in the bleachers
only yesterday.

Their faces are full of *now*. They know
the future will always be
just so. What the camera doesn't see

(or the mother, I hope,
though there's all that precedent)
is a history of drugs and booze to come,

broken marriages, despair,
reconstruction. The beautiful boys
are 70 and 60 now, both crippled,

and yet there is always that other *now*.
And this: the disasters we'd wish away
have drawn the two together.

They talk transcontinentally,
not of AA and NA as much as of
their surrogates, the Giants, the Braves,

and a world in which again and again
their teams – first one, then the other –
sweep the Series.

LOUISA'S STUDIO

High summer. Rose hips are rounding into shape,
some ruddy already behind the studio shed in which
Louisa Hopkin's sculpture (circa 1890s) has been
pushed aside by playthings: bikes, beach balls, bats . . .

An enormous, many-pointed rack from a distant elk
stretches from rafter to rafter,
bleached as drift wood, hung with hula hoops, a kite.

Louisa's naked torsos and fresh-faced children,
long gone, look down from their remove
in nooks between the studs that frame her shed.

Beyond the rose hips and loosestrife out back
on a cove-curl of beach, a bare-backed, budding girl,
also Louisa after her great grandmother, the artist,
sits facing the channel where spinnakered yachts

come and go. She has sculpted herself:
her legs and lap are covered with dark, sun-warmed
skipping stones from the beach. Her feet show
like the tips of a tail fin. She has found her niche.

HEREAFTER

If there's any hereafter it isn't enough
to stop his weeping in her closetful of
denims, cottons, silks he buries his face in,

a better service, he feels, than this
where now the priest circles her casket,
filling the empty space

with too-sweet smoke, the choir trying
to raise her on wings of Fauré's *Requiem*.
If only she could be something

more than the skin and bone he follows
to a gap in the earth. By it a huge oak has
some claim to immortality – old survivor.

What a stretching of limbs sloping down,
one resting on the sod and rising up as if
leaning on an elbow. Quickly she is

herself, one hand propping her chin,
the other reaching for a smoke in the lull
after love, its whiff still heady. Now this:

"In my father's house are many rooms" –
a pleasantly domestic view of Heaven
but insufficient.

He backs away, returns
to the digs where she waits – to breathe
her in the quilting of her comforter.

RISKING ABSURDITY

I know you're not listening
but I thought I'd tell you anyway, Mother,
how silly I feel

talking to three pounds of ash and bone grit.
Which is why I said nothing
earlier, visiting you in your city of stone

before being whisked by family
to midnight service,
the one you especially loved

where, as ever,
I was mum when the congregation
repeated the Creed, though my tongue tried
to move on its own.

Then the lights dimmed and the bells
rang midnight and the flock
knelt to sing
Stille Nächte,

after which I stepped out and saw
above bare trees
a crescent of moon rocked
by scudding clouds,

but came to. What's the moon?
Just a chunk of stone torn from the side
of the world,
steadily continuing to distance itself,

and as for *Silent Night* . . .
Still, those voices. Which is why I'm back,
Mother, risking absurdity,
having this talk.

DOCTORING

Painstakingly, I'm doctoring a family
photo in which my thin daughter is
hugging a plastic child-size skeleton
the day before the saints march in.

It's not easy, such winnowing —
so much of her is hidden
by the complicated grid of Death,
and she too bright and new a thing

for such a jumper.
I work to unveil the original pattern
and flush of her, erase a layer
of bones and the shadows they cast.

Intricately, like a surgeon removing
the tentacles of a tumor,
I delete each trace of rib and femur,
each shade, fill it all in with pinafore

and sun-warm skin. I magnify
a daughter, work slowly, pixel by pixel,
until in the end what I see — if
not what I get — is a necessary fiction.

LANDSCAPE WITH LOG CARRIER

Still here, I watch – from far off – my diminished
stick figure, the world around it immense as a winter
landscape by Li Ch'eng: wild water, jagged peaks

in which one can barely discern a tiny man
stooped under his load of sticks, his colors merging
with the muted browns and ice-blues of woods and river,

threading his way as I thread mine, bent low by logs
of ash and locust I tote up a slick path to a woodstove
fending off the elements,

my blue parka and white face not fading entirely
into shades of blue-white snow – slight hieroglyph for
Here, still here!

III. CHILD'S GARDEN

THE SECRET

Mother forbid sweets.
But my earliest memory (I was 3)
is driving down Hawthorn Street
with her to Stevers Candies

for chocolate-coated cherries
("just a few and it's only
fruit") and seeing her nick a cookie
from the Jar of Treats,

a chocolate chip, and eat it secretly
while her '36 Plymouth shimmied
at 32 and recovered at 33,
its floorboards open to the street.

In the rearview mirror I could see
her eyes revel, and knew her secret.
Later, I was pleased
to learn it was more than sweets.

A CHILD'S GARDEN
OF TERRORS

I didn't really believe Miss Ward
would tape my lips shut
if I didn't "mind my mouth."

But after school, I did
go to my Aunt Betty to be sure
it was against the rules.

She was darning a black sock
on the knob of her white "egg,"
shutting it up, as she said,

and laughed at what I told her.
When I went on too long,
silly boy, she told me dragonflies

would "zip me up" – dive down
when I babbled
and stitch my mouth

like the needle she swooped
through the dangerous air.
That night Miss Ward came at me

with the thousand eyes
of a dragonfly. Next day I was
completely mum, lockjawed.

FIRST DAY

His tongue is too thick
to round out a word he tries
for days – *sko, skoo, skooo* . . .

When it's time to
hand him over to his teacher,
he waves me off happily.

I find him later
by the swings, spilled.

The others stare, sharp-eyed

at him, head pulled in,
hands up
by his ears, legs tucked.

In the car I kiss
his wide forehead
and remember — last summer

I showed him how
a morning glory, tight shut,
dark as a bruise, if warmed

by hand and breathed upon,
springs open, blue verging
on indigo.

He had me do it over
and over. Always the miracle.
We laughed and laughed.

Now, hands cupping
his tight face, I remember
hard enough for both of us.

THE BOOK

The relief was enormous that spring of '43,
a dark time when we boys were busy
learning the silhouettes of enemy planes.

My Peepa, Mother's father, had just
"gone away," she said. I knew "died"
though I didn't want to let her know I did.
It was like babies. You didn't talk about it.
So no one could help me. I hoped

what I needed was there where the shelves
were filled with the secrets parents kept
from children, old-smelling books in a room
my father called "the den." A forbidden place,
but I was desperate . . . and yes, I found
a small volume with delicate (Chinese maybe)
drawings of the various animals
we might become when we stop being.

Or so the words I could read seemed to say
but not as clearly as the pictures,
one of a (dying maybe) man curled as a child
with a serene smile and a ghost cloud coming
from his mouth, growing into something
like a brightly colored peacock.

And I thought of the unlikely pheasant
newly come to roost in the thick pine next to
the window by my bed, hidden from view almost,
but not from a boy with a need like mine.

Even then I doubted — still, there *was* the way
the pheasant cocked his head as if to tell a really
good bedtime story.

boxes-
little place to
go to process
(ie. treehouse)

BIRTH OF A POET

It was not fashionable at Allen Creek School
for a boy to pay attention to a girl,
unless like tall Linda Bloomer
she could outrun any boy in the Sixth Grade,
in which case the proper response was to
trip her at the finish line.

Anecdotal story

pre vs post lapsarien

So when Ruthie Waymoth kissed me on a dare
on the lips, I shrugged her off, looked
to see who'd seen
and with the other guys piled on Timmy Daley
for being such a sissy. Not to be ditto
I called him names I wouldn't even call my brother.

And when I got home I climbed the white pine,
didn't stop at the safe landing of the playhouse,
arms and legs going single-mindedly
to the top of the tree, where I sat back, chewing
sap like the candy my mother warned against,

swaying in the wind
the way I'd swayed for a moment with Ruthie,
the playground far beneath us. Now
in the pine, unruly as any bird, I worked up
the first of the songs I've been singing ever since.

analogy
sexuallity = poetry

Wholebook metaphor = allegory
Smaller, but extended, metaphor = conceit

~96~

BLITZINGS

What a snow! Whiteouts on the interstates
from OH to MA, eighty plus inches on the ground in CT
and sleet on the way. The Weather Channel is delirious,
talking it up.

Their man in Pittsburgh is almost dancing with the joy
of gusts to sixty. I've had it with Jim Cantore,
the lot of them, turn off the Weather
Channel, get back to work carving a canyon to the street.

Now here I am, stalled halfway, small between snow walls
and out of gas. What business does memory have
licking its lips, kicking up its heels, reveling in 1944
when it snowed for 40 days upstate, a record said WHAM,

when even better than making Berlin out of building blocks
and bombing it to rubble with my "Flying Fortress" hands
was mushing through a blizzard with Mollie Scarf
(sent over from London in '38 before the Blitz),

reaching a seven-foot wall of heaped up snow
where the yard had once begun, and tunneling into it
as if beneath that No Man's Land of white was the world
we had in mind.

We worked our way in, advancing like moles,
digging and carting out snow to open the underground,
a shelter so impervious
no father or mother or V-2 rocket would ever find us.

SIXTEEN

After her moonlit unveiling
and mine, a Black Snake this morning,

long muscle along the limb
of a pine, bright tongue's flagrant lick,

and on a shingle of the toolshed
an Underwing moth, dark arrowhead

furred and furtive as the future
fitting into the shed's weathered cedar

but revealing beneath its upper wings
a hint of shocking scarlet and pink.

Such country matters
are suddenly illicit, best kept undercover.

In the shed's dim light, this heady
musk of tubers and seed,

sweet iron scent — like blood — of tines,
dark shine of the tools, her eyes.

SLEEPING GIANT

For the Wampano, the Sleeping Giant
was Hobbomock, who stomped so hard
on the Quinetucket, Long Tidal River,
it doglegged east to water the enemy.

Such a chest and head — but you knew
he was not, as the poet would have him,
an ogre who might wake to "rip a ditch
to pour the enemy Atlantic" into Hamden.

You were another gender and understood
there was more to your Gulliver —
for starters, the mound between his thighs
where fast girls camped.

Born just in time for Black Tuesday
and seeing how hurt from the Crash
your father was by the time you turned 12,
the report that the top of the Giant's head

had been blasted apart to quarry traprock
might have given you pause.
(You did love metaphor, a poet by nature.)
But adventure was your calling. It sent you

up the face of the Giant, Lilliputian climber
of the slick rocks lining his right temple
along the steep waterfall
cascading to the torrent that carved his chin

with a ravine you barely avoided each time,
rising rock by rock, hand over hand
to the dark quarry lake at the top of his head
where you would sit, immersed

in the guilt of feeling for the moment more
delight in your strength and youth
than sorrow for the loss of so much father
in a world too rapidly disappearing.

SHARKS AND MINNOWS

for Emily

At the family gathering in Haven Cove
the children still are children, except for her,
different this year, fourteen,
joining her parents at their remove, watching

her cousins playing Sharks and Minnows.
How quickly the minnows dash and dart
but each in turn is caught and made a shark.
Even the quickest's undone.

Now the game is called by darkness
and the sharks are civilized by baths and bed.

Next day she sets out to kayak Seal Bay
to be alone. First one cousin then others
cannot allow her departure.

They lob stones underhanded,
aiming to drench her, the stones homing.

Then one of them throws overhanded,
barely missing.

As she pulls out of range, the stoning
subsides. But not what it means. Not that.

SLAPPING THE MINT

for Gary Stow

Barebacking since childhood, extension
of a Pinto's withers, half man, half horse
he's stalled at a formal outdoor lunch,
leans back as if to pat a haunch,
picks a sprig of mint from a plot behind him,
holds it in the flat of a hand, slaps it once,
hard, and slips it in his water glass.
"Releases the flavor," he says. "Hit it just
once. Any more bruises the mint."

It's enough – I'm a child again, in love
with my large, creaturely father,
the way he roams his grounds,
hands safely behind his back in the cool
of the evening, then puts an ear to the silver
cocktail shaker he shakes just five times
so as not to "bruise the gin" in its bed
of ice and vermouth.

The gin, at least, is in luck, the way
he tends it before it ungentles him, puts
words in his mouth
in the bruising, half-animal night.

SONG OF ELPENOR

Among them all the youngest was Elpenor —
no mainstay in a fight nor very clever — and
this one, having climbed on Circe's roof to
taste the cool night, fell asleep with wine, and . . .
started up, but missed his footing on the long
steep backward ladder and fell that height
headlong. The blow smashed the nape cord,
and his shade fled to the dark. — The Odyssey, X

Always the same — another island,
another giant.
While my shipmates were busy
dealing with the latest,
I hid at the rear of his cave
in the thick of sheep,
ewes calling low in their throats
to lambs. Just fourteen, a child
myself, I understood. Beyond,

my uncle made his point, his stake
sharpened, glowing from the fire,
plunged in the eye
of Cyclops howling in sudden dark
the color of blood. The giant
became the butt of blind man's buff.

Next morning, after we slipped
through the eye of his cave,
they had to tear me
from the wool of the wether
I hid from him beneath.

Because I begged to stay behind,

called them butchers,
they made me carve a lamb alive,
forced its privates down my throat
and hauled me to the ship.

Then weeks in the bilge at an oar
before I had my liberty.

When Circe charmed the pack of us
sent to scout her place
and set us like louts to mucking out
her chicken shed,
shearing, milking, repairing walls
the boars had broken through,

I chose to herd the hogs, moved in
with them. Uncle found me at home
in mud, playing on a blade of grass
Brood Squeal, Sow Suckle.
The nephew of Odysseus back to belly
with a pig!

To make a man of me,
for the month
he bent the queen to his will, he had me
watch – pin her arms and watch.

The night before we were to sail
with whatever of hers we could,
I climbed to the roof, grew drunk on sky –
the Flying Horse, the Swan, the Eagle –

drifted off, was a child again
making wings in a rare snow, arms

sweeping, sweeping, lifting me
over the harbor boats
to circle on myself, one wingtip
steady as a compass point,
the ocean more and
more transparent,

until the boats rose up,
were quickly one boat,
the boat a foredeck,
the foredeck my
sharpening
shadow.

SONG OF THE STRIPPER

for J.G.

So I danced
mute in a haze of half-light,
borne by the white horse of oblivion,
belly, breasts and thighs about their business
of pleasing a blur of
old men.

Lap-dancing, I saw
him standing in the entryway, strobe-lit in
his favorite white suit and Panama
and knew he had come again
to take me
home,

heard him call
my name over and over my name
and when he turned for me to follow, I thought I
might, but when he looked back, his face
was too brilliant, too full
of hope.

Then the dog-faced bouncer hurled him out.
A door slammed, the dark returned and
I danced harder. But in the black
half-light between the acts
I whispered my name
my name.

DOWSER

for Ben

"I used to think better than I think
now," he says, heading out
on one of his treasure-hunting expeditions.
He looks for what's lost below

playgrounds, beaches, old foundations.
He thinks with his fingertips,
part of his brain having been removed
by scalpel and radiation.

He holds his arms before him, closes his eyes,
moves like someone in a dream, then
when his fingers tingle
he goes to his knees — and comes up

with buried rings, watches, coins, charms,
and what he loves most:
toy cars, trucks, a sand pail and shovel
that made a world some child once inhabited.

PUTTING IN THE HAND PUMP

for William Leverett.

It's time to reinstall my nemesis, the hand pump.
My twentyish grandson says "No prob"
as he follows directions I call problematic —

checks the cup leather, greases the gasket,
shuts the backflow valve, sets the "pitcher" in place,
bolts her tight, tighter, primes her with a bucketful

and pumps away,
not in the least surprised at the proper sucking sound
she makes, pulling a steel tongue in and out

of her drop pipe briskly enough for a wheeze of water
to rise up from ten feet down in the underworld.
He pumps as if he owns the water coming in huge gasps.

"You see? Simple," he says. Perhaps it's only the old —
for whom so much so seldom works — only the old
who have a proper sense of amazement.

MOMENT

Because the velvet of a black swallowtail *Butterfly*
is backdrop for such saffron dashes, indigo dots *yellow*
and two black-irised orange wing-eyes
leading to the exclamation points of twin tails,
and because it has chosen a bank of white phlox *flower*
against a rust-red barn for its setting, or rather
the lavender and light-gold heart *microcosm*
of one white flounce of phlox, and because all
of this is swaying in the morning breeze, *temporary*

a child in the garden wants more — he wants
to hold this moment in the hands he is cupping
like a net and lowering slowly, slowly over
the body of the swallowtail quivering for so much
sweetness. Should he capture it, the moment will *paradox*
be lost, and should he not, the moment will be lost,
subject change and though I'm trying to preserve it, it's being lost *metafiction*
in translation, this page merely a specimen board.
But he and I are doing what we must. *ineffable — not being able to have a word*

diminishing

RARE BOOK DEALER

Compulsion addiction

Dressed up for Halloween 75 years ago,
we stood our separate grounds,
I defending the bog side of the road,
arrow notched in my bow string,
headdress feathered, he the other side,

newly arrived, a cowboy, pistol cocked.

For years he terrified me, my speed
no defense against his slugs that bruised
more than my arms and ribs when he
leapt from the hedge along the road
I walked to school.
Every day I made plans to mollify him ...

He found me yesterday, historical
artifact at the back door,
he too in his 80s, gaunt, limping, worse
for time's wear, as beaten up as I'd been.
He showed me his find, a rare first edition
of Keats. He turned its yellowed leaves.

AT THE UPRIGHT

for Katharine Carle

You rode, devil-may-caring downhill
at 11, one knee balancing on the saddle
of your Schwinn, one leg straight back,
raucous as a jay, hands light
on the bars, considering release.

Back home you were stopped by a shot
in *Life*, July 28, 1941 – a girl your age,
mouth and eyes taut, home smoldering
behind her from a Blitzkrieg bomb.
Your eyes stung from the smoke, still do

seventy years later, so much more
of the same having hit home,
in spite of — no, because of which
you sit at your piano, the old upright,
hands still light and joyful,

playing the bars
of a song you hear from the spruce
outside your window, the notes
major and minor, of a warbler in its bower.
The bird answers you, you answer the bird.

Selections from

THE WEATHERING

I. MORNING

MORNING

Lying alone in the straight and narrow bed
of old age, I work my way down the crooked hall
of memory – to where it was I went those early mornings,
trailing behind me the tattered cloudbank of my blanket

to the room Father had not yet expelled me from,
the room with the queen-size bed and rose-red comforter
I slid under, as close to Mother as possible, molding myself
to the seed-curl of her back and shoulder, the sweet tang

of her, slowing my breathing to match her own
with long, delicious inspirations
until first light lit the cream of her neck and cheek
and day broke in

with the rustle of pheasants in the pine,
fee-bee-ing of chickadees, *phew-phew-phewing* of cardinals,
swish of washing and brushing from
the street-cleaning truck

and finally the bellsound of bottles
set in their metal basket by the Nakoma Dairy man.
And Father would groan and Mother would turn to hold
me against the soft of her,

and beyond the veil of her hair the light would grow and
she would take me by the hand along the dark crooked hall
to the back stairs, down to the brightening kitchen,
and let me bring in the milk.

I'd uncrinkle the stiff paper cap of a narrow-necked bottle,

lift the tongue on the tab beneath, pull it
from the mouth, love the liquid labor
and *pop* of its release,

and lick the cream from its underside,
the thick sweet cream,
a memory I knew — but not of what.

AND GOD BLESS HARRY

After I godblessed everyone
and mother left
I godblessed Harry Walker

because when the air raid siren
wailed and Miss Berger rushed us
past Harry saluting
from the furnace room

and lined us up
and made us sit small as we could
and hug our knees,

I knew the Luftwaffe wouldn't
because Harry winked at me
and made circles around his ear.
And he would know —

the way he did when Miss Berger
sent me to the principal
for doodling in math

and Harry stiff-armed his *Heil*
with a push broom under his nose
and a wicked grin for principals.

The last time I saw Harry Walker
they had him in a crib.
He couldn't move a thing.

But his eyes made circles
and I knew he had them licked.

BAPTISM

after "Baptism in Kansas," John Steuart Curry

Things keep going on the way they do
except one day in the middle of nothing
they don't.

I remember how hot it was – not a creak
from the windmill
and the Fords our folks had come in
steamed.

We stood around.
Our pockets were no place for hands,
they said, and wouldn't let us in the dark
of the barn or anywhere God wouldn't be
because the preacher was in the yard
to baptize whoever he could
in Tatums' water tank.

Six lined up.
I envied them the cool of their gowns
and the year or so they had on me
but not the way he dragged them under
and kept them there so long they bucked
like bullheads.

Mostly, I went along with the hymnbook
someone pushed at me
until he got to Ellen McGee,
held her under and didn't stop,
thinking maybe anything that pretty
was bound for goings on.

I was ready for something like the cat
I had tried to drown and failed
when up she came as sweet . . .
and stood for a spell at the edge
of the tank, at home in the sky.

And her gown, wet through, was true to her
and her face was where the sun had been.

THE ZENITH

for Brendan Burns and Jesse Case

Always the tall dark of the barn
to hide in, the mattressing
alfalfa, timothy, meadow grass.

Beyond the hickory stanchions
smooth as well-worked leather
from a century and more of cows,

beyond the Jerseys,
their mouths full of summer,
I climb a ladder to the haymow,

from there to the cupola, a rope.
Like any raccoon I settle down.
It all comes in clearly now:

a gabbling of frogs in the swamp,
a whippoorwill in the pines,
June bugs banging the Coleman

and maybe 50 stations on a Zenith,
an old one shaped like a church
I've resurrected tube by tube.

Wired to the milk shed, grounded
on the hand pump, it brings in
the Tigers, the Indians, the Pirates.

One by one I call them up,
in touch with everywhere.

THE NAMING

The summer I was twelve I began to know
the "Bottom" – old growth sycamores and locusts
thick with furred and gnarling vines.
I dug root-raftered burrows in mud-hole banks,
bushwhacked my way

to a clearing and something more,
bark on its logs, guinea hens on its roof,
a sow with one eye open under it,
and rocking on the stoop, smiling crookedly

at the little savage come up from the Bottom,
a man who said *Huh*. That summer I learned
to grain the guineas, slop the hogs,
kick the sow in the snout for chewing my boot,

bait hooks with crayfish, pull in bullheads,
slice off their barbs
and gut them with a single scoop of the hand.
I wore a crow's feather in my hair,
sometimes a cat bird's, once an oriole's,

told no one how Henry Minor taught me
to fox-bark,
fire only once, and when the fox ghost hovered,
ask of it a blessing.

Then school began and he got work
raising a suspension bridge between two states.
When he returned, he slurred

and turned away.

By now I was occupied with being thirteen
too much to mind. Who was he anyway?
Some drunken Indian. He deserved
the bottle-bomb I set off in his outhouse.
When he fired at me, I couldn't forgive him.

Or myself. Or whoever tore down his shack.
Or how he vanished and fifty years passed
before he surfaced in the obit it took
for me to start forgiving. It's time I called him
by his proper name –

Cries Like A Fox, come from where you hide
at the wood's edge – let me bless you, be blessed.
Father, name me, tell me who I am,
give me back my feather
of Crow, feather of Cat Bird, feather of Oriole.

THE PASS

Plato put it well, like so:
beyond the particular is the permanent.
That is, beyond the arc of one dead jay I throw
to the woods (it hits a pine and drops),

beyond such a broken arc and all the others –
like the almost parabolic piss I took at recess

and hit the drinking fountain and got sent
to Miss Ward.

Beyond such arcs
is the one they all aim to be.
I think I saw it in November of '53.
It was the Blue against the Brighton 2's,
fourth quarter, tight,
when Number 3, George Nichols of the Blue

faded back in the mud, back
to the end of his own end zone
and got one off as he went down. It spirals still
to the 50 and into the arms of the wide end
who fakes and cuts and pulls it in, a peach.
He hardly has to look for the ball.

Behind him Nichols is down, his number's mud,
but what he threw
was just what Plato knew he would.

HOME BURIAL

A boy is in the field, digging a hole,
whose father has been stunned by
the sledge of time, doesn't know

enough to drop or try again.
A boy is in the field, digging
a hole which is perfectly square,

whose father makes nothing true,
not his crooked furrows, swayback
barn, pretty wife.

A boy is in the field, digging
a hole which is perfectly square,
knowing all,

whose father didn't know enough
to keep old Moses from
bloating himself on half-ripe oats,

couldn't find the slugs
to shoot the horse
and had to use a maul.

A boy is in the field, digging
a hole which is perfectly square,
knowing all too well

how his mother once swung him
flat out in the spinning world
and said she'd never let go, ever.

A boy is in the field, digging
a hole which is perfectly square,
knowing all too well who it was

he saw,
skirt up in the mow
with the hired man.

A boy is in the field, digging

a hole which is perfectly square,
knowing all too well all he can do

is make it deep,
straight down enough
for more than a stiff-legged horse.

LINES

for R.W.

It's only glass
I've broken. Mother goes on
licking a thread, pushing it at the eye,
face bunching like a club,
then heaves out of her chair and begins

to hit me
with a magazine, and when that shreds,
with her fists.

I can't forgive my father
for hiding
behind the paper, a big man twice
her size. As usual, he lets her happen,

doesn't say a thing.
She does the talking in that house.
My father is her cross, she says.
I can't forgive him
for not knowing better

and hide in the shed among the tools.
Today, he comes for me, has nothing
to say, just shows me
to the car. We reach the river,

and in the trunk beside his rod
I find a brand new Heddon Tru-flex
with a Shakespeare reel. From his tackle
he selects a Green Ghost and
Royal Coachman.

How delicately, with a huge hand
battered and missing a finger, he threads
the silk through the shining eyes.

All afternoon we work the trout.
The only sounds
are those that slowly grow used to us
and the high song, long whisper
of lines.

First his, then mine, then sometimes
together, the lines arch out and settle
exactly where we want them.

MY FATHER'S STORY

One of his hands held the pulpit hard,
grew livid every Sunday.
The other aimed at the faithful.

Back and forth it would rake us,
mowing us down.

Like Abraham with Isaac overhead
my father held the Host, then broke it.
The wafer, snapping, might have been
me, held up, an example.
Of course it wasn't. It was God.
Over and over God broke
beneath his hands.

Nothing stood up to him.
When a cougar stopped our Franklin
ten miles beyond Carmel,
slow as the switch of the animal's tail
he reached for the tool box
on the running board, and the cat
backed off, didn't like the looks
of a hand that righteously raising
a hammer.

Moving east in '15, held up by snow
in the Sierras, my first,
we all got down from the Pullman.
I said I was an angel and could prove it.
Flat out, I made wings in the snow
and sang the Alleluiah Chorus.

When I turned to take my punishment
there were iceballs in both his hands
and one in the air above.
He was juggling, juggling snow,
as sure of where we were as any angel.

MY FATHER'S HANDS

After work when the big and little hands
pointed opposite ways, he would listen
to the silver cocktail shaker he shook
just enough not to *bruise the gin*
and would down his three martinis.

Promptly at seven, dinner. A good wine
and he'd warm to the stories he told
more fashionably than any conversation.
Then Bach, his fingers
trembling on the strings, eyes closed,

after which he would disappear
behind the evening paper, the obits,
looking for news of his larger family,
the hundreds who worked for him.
If only I did, I thought,

making myself small, trying not to think
how long it took him to see me
through the amber of a single malt
and tell me *Later*. Some nights he would
come to my room,

instruct me
with parables from his own boyhood,
knead my shoulders, ribs, the small
of my back – knead them sternly as if he
might be able to reform me.

SIGNS

Beyond my father,
splendid in his Lincoln Zephyr
making time cross country,
were the signs – a sign for caverns

miles deep where fish had whiskers
for eyes and we'd get lost
and I'd save us with my length
of string, and one for Dinosaur Valley

where the bones would rise up
with backs like the Rockies
and tails to bash whoever I wanted.
"Couldn't we stop?"

Never. But I loved him desperately.
My head on his lap beneath the wheel,
his thigh muscle flexing, I saw
him enter the ring

in scarlet tails and a black top hat.
He flicked his whip
and two by two introduced things
too terrible not to be true.

WAR NEWS

At breakfast with father,
when I grew tired of seeing the war news
on the back of the paper he held, bare-
knuckled, I studied what else stood between us.

For all its British silver, it was Byzantine
and Gallic, onion-domed
and perforated with tiny fleurs-de-lis to
pour the sugar.

Or so I say now —
back then it was merely beyond me.
And he went on flipping pages with angry snaps.
Nothing worth his while there.

Still, the paper stayed up, the test
continued. I thought
of snatching *The Times* away, finding
my father

less furious
than disappointed I was, as ever,
stupid, stupid, stupid — like all the rest that
passed for news. So I waited,

watched his hand emerge, huge
and graceful,
close around the sugar tower,
raise it deftly out of sight behind the paper,

sweeten,
and return it, ridged and shining,
to its appointed place.
I made a promise to myself:

I would study harder,
craft myself more perfectly, wait patiently
for him to notice and reach out
that gently to me.

THE UNDOING

I jump from crosstie to crosstie,
walk the humming rails
I've been warned against
high over nothing, no net below

the trestle, and farther along
come face to face with a barn
through which the tracks run on,

a heavyset barn, row of dark panes
like unbroken eyebrows
above the open double doors.

Within, I'm lost,
hands tied to a post, shirt off,
pants down,

and his belt slipping through
the loops, its slap against a palm

like stropping a razor, its whisper,
hiss and crack.
What little I am is less . . .

Then there's no one, no buckle
shining like a badge, just the flash
of swallows, white of droppings.
The barn's roof is sagging,
slates broken.

I open a toolbox I'm never to open
and see no tools,
just thick red sticks I set so well
that when I trigger the barn
the fall of debris is gentle, a good
growing rain.

MOVING MOTHER

birth / rebirth

Every spring she began again
to do her hair, legs curled beneath her,
nude at the heart of the garden,
flush terra cotta too much the image
bronze statue *personal*
of my mother. Not for friends to see.
I was in favor of fall, leaves hiding parts
of her, and at last the removal,
but hated the way my father held her,

down

taking her to the cellar, the pitch
black she wintered in — except for one

winter / darkness "death"

mica eye of the furnace
blazing, throwing light darkly on her.

What did I know? After he willed her
to me, I took her home
too carelessly, broke off a foot, a hand.

It's time I reconsidered
how she nestled in his arms.

[handwritten annotations: "shiny silver" with arrow pointing to "mica", "warmth" above "furnace", "child" above "What", "comfort?" to the right, "terra cotta statue" below]

II. ORDINARY ANGELS

TWELVE

for Robin

A pretty good day, junk fish
and a couple of trout.
Friendly with muskrat
I drift, I cast at rings,

pass the '58 Chevy with fins,
stripped, a place to play
in which I once found
underthings.

What's up
around the bend
is flowers, and among them,
reaching for the sky,

legs,
some girl's, toes curling,
curling, nails red, her fur
a sight. The boy I forget.

CECROPIA

It wasn't butterflies I went for, such daily flirts,
but moths, the shy ones, furred and thick-fronded,
pale green, lavender, umber, and rose-mottled
giants signed with the Eye of God.
Polyphemus, Promethea, Luna, Io, Cecropia.

Luring such mystery with a lantern
the summer I was thirteen, I saw across the street
the bride, moon-white, bridesmaids pale green
dancing in the gold and navy night.

At sixteen I harbored a harem of cocoons, silk-
sacks swelling, also a '51 Victoria convertible,
cow-horned, coral red.

The day I was licensed I floored her
on NY 96, Peggy Carlson drumming our song
on the dash. Gearing down for the turn
onto Kreag, I backfired and backfired for Peggy,
who rose, leaned into the wind like a sprit,
her arms in the air in a V and her fingers V's
and the plunge of her two-piece – oh lord!

When I pulled in, late, a Cecropia had hatched,
was half eaten by ants.
They blackened its bright new body,
the sockets where eyes had looked for some way
out of this, the pink and umber wings,
too wet to fly.

SOLSTICE

At the instant of Solstice, when the sun stands still, all things are said
to be at that Moment of Equilibrium when an egg will stand on end.

Nothing stands still this Solstice dawn.
Light lengthens on the bedroom ceiling, assuming
the form of a wide-winged ✝

with a bright amber square at its crux.
What physics is this? I'm used to Platonic
shadows: black wings, dark branches.

The boy in me sees a balsawood P-40.
But the Old Believer says it's the Holy Cross,
its core a terrible brilliance of open heart.

Now the post of the Cross is dividing,
dividing again, becoming two sets of legs,
and the cross piece is doubling, might be

a pair of arms blessedly combining
with another pair of arms. All's in motion
toward the very moment time will stop —

the legs shudder, and under such a ceiling
her eyes grow brighter, take me in.
From the heart of us a light less amber than

citron, less citron than gold, is simplifying
whatever was merely human
until nothing is left of us but illumination . . .

which slowly grows fainter — lets us down
like anything perfectly upright declining after
its Moment of Equilibrium.

LEARNING THE ANGELS

Waiting up, he's deep in *Angels and Archangels,*
studying lion-bodied Cherubim, Principalities

six-winged, translucent as cathedral windows,
heavily armored Archangels, and ordinary

angels for the dirty work, recording, hand-
delivering, and as he learns, placing a finger on
the lips of every newborn, leaving a cleft
imposing silence concerning clouds of glory.

Now she breezes in, douses the light, wants
to cuddle, undoes, runs a finger along the cleft
that gives the tip of his sex its face of a heart.
It's devil's work, he knows.

But here he is in the dew-damp garden at dawn
picking strawberries for her,
turning the leaves pale-side-up, uncovering
the heart-shaped fruit

and coming on the snake, a hog-nose, head up,
neck flared and glistening. He knows its lineage,
says his prayer
to angels, archangels and wheels of fire.

Reinforced, he returns
full of Powers and Dominions. She yawns,
half rises on her divan, plumps a pillow,
pours cream on the berries. Its blush

deepens. He finds himself sliding a hand
beneath her robe,
along the nape, the shoulders, the spine,
the small, that valley lightly downed

which leads to what comes over him,
her shoulder blades working the air,
her finger on his lips.

RENDEZVOUS IN
A COUNTRY CHURCHYARD

I'm early. I sit on Timothy Cowles,
d 1788, ae 41, and wait.
She'll be here soon:
the sun's not long for this world.
Meanwhile, Char ty How rd
depa t d in   r 3 th yr
is disappearing from her stone.

Over the Hales and Hopes,
the sons and daughters of the above,
their spouses and relicts,
sugar maples are all a mumble,
might be saying prayers for the dead,
except it's caterpillars:
the trees are half eaten, food for
worms with their prattle of scat
raining from leaf to leaf.

The usual mockingbird is at his
vireo, his bobolink and cardinal,
such pretty lies – like my lady's lips,
her eyes, the skull's dress-up.

But soft, she comes, her lantern lit,
her face a lie I willingly accept.
She has me believing
the mockingbird's latest
is the very song of Charity Howard
delighting with Timothy Cowles.

END OF THE SEASON

Scraping bottom, I pole us,
two old-timers,
through the gut to Pickerel Cove.
Within, it's stop and go
and stinks. No place to bring you.

"Think how it was in the spring,"
I say – clear, the big snappers
gliding up like ocean-going Greens,
Pileateds scalloping the shoreline
red, white and black,
draping swags from tree to tree.

Whatever's left now is on its way
out – water lilies shut, olive drab
sepals stiff, a half-pint flask half
under, two mud-brown bobbers
mired –

all too apt. I'm at a loss, my love,
ship the paddle,
let the marbled algae have its way.

Is that you humming?
You like something so far gone?
I like how you chime in
with the splay-legged frogs
chirping, careening the scum,

how you let a slime of duckweed

and ooze of late bog-spawn
slide through your fingers

like a miser forgetting to count,
and how you sniff, connoisseur
of stinks.

But what do you make of this
that rises darkly to starboard now,
tows the swamp-green barge
of a shell, dangles the dead head
of a water lily from jagged jaws,
inhales hoarsely

and sinks, slowly
until only the algae on its shell
protrudes like quills?

We know the stories —
mergansers, mallards, cygnets
going under with barely a ripple.

What you do
is reach out to rub it
with your paddle, and the old
snapper rubs back, revolving
so slowly counterclockwise
we lose track of time.

Next thing it's dusk. In the still
of the gut, the rushes,

feathered beige, almost lavender
in the last light,
brush my neck, shoulders,
bare arms.

I like how you smile, reach back
to dub me with your paddle.

DAWNING

Reflecting the moonshine glittering
from a brewing bogful of peepers penny-whistling
and the fen toad's *woo-ah woo-ah* all night,

these two slip into sleep and out of themselves,
on tour, appearing in the dreams of one another.
When the nightly show is closed
by morning's pewter, blue, and lavender dove-song,

he feels the press of her finger on his lips
forbidding a word
in this new world only half removed from the other,
here on this cumulus of sheet and pillow

from which he looks up – into the coming
of her eyes. About her disarray of hair, first light.

CEREMONY, INDIAN SUMMER

an anniversary song

The afternoon ripens, the whippoorwill
begins. Two dragonflies pause,
yellow-striped, red-tipped on a snag,
then blur to the pond,

resume their ritual, arched bodies coiled
tail to head and head to tail,
an eight-winged wheel of fire, a figment
from Ezekiel

above the bridal dance
of cloud-white, wing-furred caddis flies
redoubled by the pond.
Thistle seed drifts like confetti.

And deeper down in the angling light
past nubile perch in green and saffron
shallows, a pair of three-foot carp seem lit
from within

the color of the lingering sun,
their roiling in the rising mist of spring,
backs humped half out, snake-sinuous,
forgotten. The stillness of the carp

is so complete each red-gold, black-lined
scale shines separately, the pulse of tail fins
oriental, like the sway of night into day
into night.

AN OLD MAN'S SENSE

of time is shot. Now he is five in Indian headdress
facing off with the boy across the street
and now he is being born. The frames

blur by – his small head crowning, coming to light
is an old man's, white on hospital
white. Now the film so quickly reeling and unreeling

jams. It fixes on a single frame.
Before a brilliant circle burns out from its center,
he sees

a sleeping compartment
elegant in the velvet and brass-fitted style
of the overnight express from Algeciras to Madrid.

He is raising a tasseled, dark green window shade
on the full Spanish moon. The white of it spills
across the cream and umber landscape of his bride.

III. SUDDEN WEATHER

THE RAISING

Already four retaining walls are standing against
the tide. The builders have molded
the Temple of Eros and beyond it the Pyramid
of a Thousand Steps. When the sea rises

they rush to shore the outer wall.
The more beach-goers gape at "two grown men
doing that," the more the couple's passion grows
for the laying on of sand.

It's a calling, like the part I play beneath
such accumulating clouds – the prophet pointing
overhead, declaring "Atlantis Delenda Est.
Oh, Truth and Beauty, whither goest?"

For their part, the builders cover their ears
operatically. Now the sky over South Beach goes
black, wind quickens, and thunderheads flare up
with a familiar fury these two take to heart,

abandoning all irony for their pièce de résistance:
a Byzantine dome encircled with what
appear to be flamboyant seraphim, swords raised.

SUDDEN WEATHER

I can live with hurricanes,
their predictable haunts,
habits, established names.

But what of that other sort
of storm, that blackness
out of the blue,

whiplash of wind,
end of more
than power?

And what of us? Against
whatever fury
brews in you for days

I lay in provisions, secure
all entryways.
I ride out rage, remain.

It's sudden weather
in the midst of love
will be the end of us.

Epiphany : Sudden Realization

BREAK UP

for D. W.

It's a godsend, this winter thaw,
I tell my brother, long distance.
He answers such warmth's unnatural.

When he asks how long it's been
since she left me, I'd say I have no idea
but am interrupted by a rumbling

from Smuggler's Notch. Which grows.
Now, where the creek clears the ridge,
trees are cracking

and a blue-white flash flood
of break-up ice cuts through,
shaking the house,

leaving a stand
of river birch in ruins beneath a wrack
of ice that glitters jade and silver.

When I can hear again, I hear more
clearly the small voice on the other end.
"Forever," I say, "she's been gone forever."

She was never really there

IN THE VALLEY

Mold and mildew. Beneath the kitchen sink
long pink and white shoots, beige-furred,
grow out of the eyes of Golds and Idahos.
The doorbell's dead, the pipes are bleeding
blue in the tubs, the water pump keens,
the roof leaks, the whole house is going soft.
I take it personally.

There's also the business of the light
in the upstairs hall
where the family is hung, two whole rows
of framed stiffs
coming out, coming down the aisle, going off
to war. No doubt the fixture I've just installed
will overheat like the last one
and with a sizzle and flash leave our forebears
in the dark. So it goes.

While I wait for Sharples the Chimney Man
to return, let me fill you in. A week ago
our Little Godin began to smoke us out
but before the coal gas caused total obscurity
Sharples fixed us up with a 5-inch connector
and a 9-foot extension that towers over the house
like the Newark incinerator — and doesn't work.

What else but retreat to *The Valley of Horses*?
Better Ayla than the flickering Zenith
where balding barbershoppers are carrying on,
crooning *Kiss me once and kiss me twice* . . .

Thank God, he's back. Sharples.
He inserts a gauge in the stovepipe
to register the draft, and shakes his head.
"Minus 2, minus 6, you have a negative draft," he says.
"Doesn't make sense," he says. "She should draw
like a Hoover." And here's the rub:
"You must be in a natural low pressure zone."
I knew it.

He kneels before the stove,
says it's never happened to him before, pops a pill
from a bottle in his socket wrench box, departs,
does something on the roof
and reappears. He wads up paper, lights her,
and lo, we have to back off before she sucks us in.

It seems he has over-corrected. What to do
is his business. Mine is *The Valley of Horses*
where everything's new — and works.
So far Ayla has invented Fire, the Wheel,
and the Beast of Burden.
Just now she's about to invent,
with the first man she comes upon . . .

Before she can, my daughter walks in
with her young man. Interruptus once again.
He wants to call somewhere. I tell him to watch
the phone jack: it pulls out (how often I've lost
my party). "You have to click the tab on the jack,"
he says, with the patience of youth.

All right, I'm senile.
But when I've finished over-paying Sharples,

I add it all up:

one light fixture, illuminating for the moment,
a working phone, a coal stove in the pink.
I can see, I can hear, I can feel – therefore I am,
I think I am, though the Zenith still flickers.

ADMISSION

for Sarah

From the blind of my dream I watch
a latter-day Susanna bathe. The whites of
her teeth glitter, her dark secret fur

glistens. Then the otherworldly wail
of something
calls me

back to you beside me in bed,
your cries subsiding, the pain that stunning.
Now at St. Francis

Emergency, you bite your lip, eyes wide.
A young intern pulls up your gown.
"Does this hurt, or this?"

he asks, splaying your legs, pressing hard
where they meet.
A sharp cry seems to please him.

I know, it's his job.
And mine is strangling him . . .
until I'm called back to you, and again

am diverted — by rain lashing, wind keening,
jumbo jets tossed about, unable to land
according to the anchor on Channel 2.

What can anchor me?
I place a compress on your brow, change it,
concentrate on not composing this,

unsuccessfully. There is no health
in me. For which I hear the gurney coming to
cart me off to the underworld, but of course

it comes for you. They tape your ring,
explain the muscles relax under anesthesia,
rings fall off. More likely good pickings,

I think, and try to remember what ring
cynics are consigned to
and how much ring-loosening I'm guilty of.

Be true to her,
I want to tell the nurse who delivers
preliminary oblivion. His name tag says

"Angel." With that hush hush voice he's too
otherworldly. For one who doesn't believe
in signs, I'm surprisingly terrified.

How quickly you could go into the dark
like the moon torn from Earth or this bright new
galaxy collapsing into the hole at its heart,

I write, cannot stop writing,
when what I want is to pray:
Please hold the instruments steady for her.

And now it's time to wait. I will be true . . .
But when they return you, *they* are all
you need, they and the morphine-trickler

you fondle between your breasts and squeeze,
making the trickler chime like
a fasten-seat-belt sign in one of the jumbos.

Sleet rattles the window, and I remember
your long approach is far from sure.
Come in, my love, come in.

THE BALANCING

Rome: December, 1985

On his own this morning, lugging his bags
to the check-in counter, he is just another
of her numbers. She works here
as a Balancer, measures baggage against jet fuel.

He clenches his eyes, relives last night:
how she came back from the airport, late,
how he wanted her,
how she knocked his hands away in fury,
how he shot back. Now this.

He looks up, must be the last to know.
The arrival and departure screens are riddled,
glass crackles underfoot,
a pattern of blood designs the wall.

At Security the carabinieri carry Uzis.
No one says a thing. On board, they frisk
each other's faces.

It fills the papers: there were four,
back to back in a circle.
They weren't particular about their targets.

He turns a page, sees Mohammed Sharam,
the youngest, quoted as saying
gunmen dragged his father from a loom
in Gaza, cut off both hands,

and while his sister knelt, head down
as if to Mecca, raped her.

The wheels slam into the belly of the plane.
It rises above the city, which simplifies, is lost.
The world turns white,
then silver, pale blue, reminding him
of the ice on Pemadumcook. He'll go there —
little cabin, nice fire. Cold nights the ice
explodes, but it harbors no fury,
no national cause. When a floe scrapes a floe
it sounds like cellos.

Still there is no peace.
From where she works, she must have seen it
all, must have come home to
rest her head on him, whisper "No, oh God, no!"

Balanced between the old world and the new
near the point of no return, he turns
toward her, heads home.

THE DIGGING

It's that time of year,
the hedgerows hung with bittersweet.
Potato time.

How early the freeze, I'd say
if we were speaking. We're not.
We turn our spading forks against

the earth. It's stiff,
the Reds and Idahos hard as stone,
a total loss.

Once it was us against the beetles,
blight, whatever was not potato.
How they flowered, rows and rows

in white. Now look.
We give it one last try, and there
far down in softer soil,

a seam of them, still perfect.
One after another
we hold them up to the dying day,

kneel down to sift for more.
In the dark of earth, I come upon
your hand, you mine.

RETROSPECTIVE

So many takes of Jo at Hopper's retrospective —
they say he married her for a permanent model.
Jo as hooker, nipples rouged, hair flaming with henna;
Jo hunched at a counter, night hawking;
Jo as wolf girl crawling into bed, nether fur licked
by the lecherous wind,
or naked at a gaping flophouse window.

Once, happily, she's Pierrette,
white ruff at neck and wrists, receiving applause
she deflects with a deprecating gesture of her hand
toward Pierrot, clearly Hopper himself
who touches his chest
as if before he can bring himself to respond

he feels an old weakness of the heart
keep him remote as the coast of Maine he loves
the way she wishes to be loved, wishes
so terribly she rages
in silence. I understand. I too have earned such
rage you keep to yourself, my dear, as we go on
from Hopper to Hopper.

Now from a dark place behind *Two Comedians*
where a film shows every half hour,
a loud thud
is followed by the ascending laceration
of a scream rising into a gasped series of *No's.*
Then the silence that follows a natural disaster.

Across the gallery your face is unmasked
in a shock so pure
it's a mirror for mine. How long
it has been since we looked at each other
so – not husband, not wife,
but true as only strangers thrown together are.

IV. WE ALL FALL DOWN

HOME BIRTH

for Ben

The cord was about your neck
when you were born
blue. A blizzard was raging.

You survived, and the weather
turned, but today spring snow
drifts high as the bird feeder

where the cat digs in, hunkers,
and deep in her throat makes
bird noise: ruffles, clever trills.

The birds know, except a junco
comes close, too close.
The cat leaves it for me to end.

When I turn to you
my shadow darkens the crib.
You sound too like the bird.

I look elsewhere,
concentrate on the egg shine
of dawn I woke to this morning,

magnified wings silhouetted
on the window shade, worldly
celestials: starlings

in love with construction,

scratching snow from the gutter,
weaving a wattle of twigs, doing their

parody of whatever deconstructs —
rattle of snow plow, snarl of chain saw,
birdcall of cat. Such a razzing!

May a starling be your totem, Ben.
May you not be taken in, rise above false
ruffles and trills, mock the Destroyer.

WE ALL FALL DOWN

for Kelly, my student

Her turn had come. She knew
by heart almost
the lines she was to speak
but gave us, God help her,

the truth
beyond the lines,
beyond the book she dropped,
its pages thrashing to the floor
like broken wings —

the truth
she beat her head upon,
bit into so hard
I could not pry her jaws,
teeth grinding —

the truth beyond us
she saw as ever,
her risen eyes gone white
as bone.

I did what I could,
I held her and held her, seized
with sudden love and knowing
we all fall down.

In the end
I carried her curled in my arms
across one threshold
and another.

BEYOND THE MYSTIC

for Beeke and David

He began building the boat when doctors gave me
a year, maybe two.

He used nothing but the best – bronze bolts,
white oak for the battens and gussets,
ironwood for the keel.

Now, in the cool of evening, I ride
my name on the prow,
listening to the intermittent ping of the fish scanner.
We work a pair of poles.

He is taking me down the Mystic
to his favorite haunts, celebrating contradiction.

As we pass beneath the 99th St. Bridge,
the big trucks making their metallic thunder
on the perforated steel of the roadway above,
he selects another lure,
the lamp on his head less a miner's than a surgeon's —

the big one he pulls up amazingly
from such a place
will be a mystery, like perfect health.
Nothing doing, no bites . . .

A year, maybe two — time for my marrow to turn
white, bones riddled and cracking.

Now, where the Mystic opens
into Boston Harbor, we move on to deeper water
beside the Chelsea Power Station's
screech of steam, and pass a foaming spill
of superheated water. It draws the Blues, he says.

From the plant's many stacks
cold white, pale green, and deep red beacons pulse,
reflecting on the thickening mist and tidal eddies,
multiplying strangely. A searchlight scans the scene
like the pointer on an x-ray screen. Just beyond,

by a flood-lit construction site and the clattering
of scrap metal on a recycling plant's conveyor belt,
he has a strike, pulls in a striper, mauve-streaked,
not quite a keeper.

It has swallowed the lure. He cuts the leader,

holds the fish over the side of the boat,
waits for a sign of life,
holds it a long time in the healing water.
I want to tell him

Let go,
I am not what I was
but I am
what I will be,
waiting for you, always here
just beneath the surface.

LOCKSMITH

Beyond the boarded up Richfield station
with its crumbling porte cochère
and old glass-headed pumps, a sign:
Clocks & Toys Repaired,
Locksmithing. And underneath,
in finer blue and red, *Country Quilts.*

He lets me in through the kitchen,
gray-grizzled paunch
too much for his terry cloth robe.
Dishes overflow the sink.

He takes my suitcase, leads me
through the parlor.
In the half dark, an open couch-bed,
someone in it.

Downstairs, his shop is immaculate,

a place where everything will work –
clocks, watches, bits of a tiny carousel
laid out precisely on a workbench.

Next to them, a jeweler's eyepiece.
Pulling up a chair to the suitcase
he whistles happily, runs a hand across
its hardware, shines a pen light on it,
darkens: "She's a Marathon. Tough case."

He jiggles a tool in the lock,
shakes his head,
takes key after key from a box, holds them
up to the light, shakes his head again, rises,
goes to a rack, runs a finger slowly down
his "blanks,"

pauses, reverses direction, and stops
at the space where the right one should be,
continues to point as if it might appear,
says that's the way it is – nothing he can do.

Returning, we pass through the parlor.
No sound from the bed, no definition,
but on the wall behind, a portrait
with its own small light –
dark hair, high cheekbones, green eyes
above a quilted shawl.

"Cancer," he says. "Two months, maybe three."

From the dark of the driveway, I see him
enter the workroom, pick up the eyepiece,
put it down,
turn again to the wall of blanks.

LAST

in the Kuznetsk Alatau Mountains, Southern Siberia

[handwritten: Tense]

He and she are old. They are dying. They make
no sense, are in the way, a remnant
no longer protected by their valley's deep pocket
to which the oil rigs have come, and drillers from Kiev,

[handwritten: extinction]

whose word for them means "loco locals."
He's bent like a Siberian birch from
too many winters. And she at ninety a chanter of the old
songs – in a language these two are the last to speak.

No matter. No one needs the word
for *pine smoke-fire for orchard frost*. Diesel smudge pots do it
better. And sixty-one nouns for healing herbs *[handwritten: Out dated]*
are pointless. The world has pharmaceuticals.

[handwritten: change]

This is the way evolution works. It doesn't protect
what isn't needed, wipes it out, tries
something else, obliterates that,
starts again . . .

Evolution has no use for the senseless song
she sings, cradling him at the foot of the apple ladder
from which he has fallen, or for a love-name he prolongs
unintelligibly, tracing like a blindman the map

of her palm, map unauthorized by the authorities, map
containing delights that only these two remember,
map that he holds onto, even as his hand
falls away from hers. *[handwritten: Death]*

SO MUCH MOURNING

is unreasonable they say,
taking me where fish shacks
bloom on the ice
turquoise, pink, jade,

and this year's contestants
tie lures to lines to flash
like chandeliers in the dark
fish parlors,

inviting the big one,
the winner,
and the young go at it
in GMC's rocking the ice.

All I hear is a drumming
below, hollow thud of waves
on a ceiling of ice: someone
trapped beneath a final lid.

I know — the ice will relent,
be a dazzle of lake, bluegills
in fish shack colors will jump.
But not now, not yet.

for Margy

THE MUGGING

She runs so hard she leaves herself behind:
high heels, a hat and coat line the sidewalk.
The catch is, she's chasing the mugger.

He's lanky, raw, could outrun her easily
but not the way he ducks and dodges
as if the enemy
is everywhere, as if the street is mined.

When she grabs his shirt, he waves her purse,
white flag.
She follows through, knocks him
into the path of a bus.

Now two cops are trying to raise her
where she kneels,
his head in her arms, all around her a spill
of belongings, his and hers. Nothing moves.

She and the man her hair half hides
are white as marble.

WILDFLOWERS

for Jocie

After visiting you, raised up on the bed
to breathe, the only color in your face
the dark of an open mouth

and a spot on the lower lip
where you must have bitten yourself;

after searching the whites of your eyes,
conceiving of your mind as blank
and admitting that nothing
will color it in,

I've come out here to remember you
in the field you loved. In vain.
What was it you saw in these flowers?
They're all show,
hypocrites and liars, lippy little flirts.

Or worse, they're not, they're dying –
like the Queen Anne's Lace,
your favorite: blank white faces,
black spots at the heart,
that just a week ago were green cups
to catch the rain and hold the dew.

I'm wrong, of course. In a quick wind
the lace begins to sway, white gone
to shades of cream and pink and pale blue.
The dark at the center is Tyrian.

I'm bringing a handful to put by your bed.
It has a lovely scent,
like carrot. You'll remember.

V. THIS

SISTER MARIE ANGELICA
PLAYS BADMINTON

with Sister Marie Modeste most afternoons.
Today, because of lengthy vespers, they are late.
A pale moon has already risen and early bats
are darting like black shuttlecocks.

Except for the whisper of wings
and the Sisters' hushed encouragement,
the only sounds are the plinking of rackets
and a monotone of mourning doves.

On all sides of the court
the sculpted yew in cubes and columns
might pass for black so deeply green it grows.
And now it moves closer,

Marie Angelica would say,
who has been known to have visions.
Though she moves as aptly as the bats,
doesn't miss a shot,

when she fades for a long one
from Marie Modeste, sways on her toes, arches
her back, raises one arm
and the other to keep her difficult balance,

she is lost, a long-legged girl again
in mare's tail, mullein, milkweed,
leaning on the sudden sky as if it can sustain her
like a hand in the small of her back. It does.

Her nerve ends quick as a shiver of poplar,
arms like branches in a wind,
she feels a cry begin
to rise, to force the self before it

and burst, all colors one. That white.
It vaults straight up, a feathered cry
that hovers in the heart of heaven, hovers,
and plummets to the gut

of the racket she sights it in,
the perfect bird, the shuttlecock
Marie Angelica keeps in play, will not let fall
despite the darkness gathering.

THE REVEREND ROBERT WALKER SKATES

on Duddingston Loch at sunset
in black — black top hat and frock coat,
britches, garters, stockings, skating shoes
black. Except for pink laces
and the flush on his face, slightly deeper
at the ears,
he is black as this morning's sermon.

Oh yes, his scarf is white. And if I say the ice
is black, I mean it's not, is in fact
a window for fish.

The Reverend has turned his back on the sky
between the hills, which is the color of his ears.

His right leg is raised, extends behind him
like the long tail feathers of some exotic bird.
He is leaning into the wind,
leading with the sharpened blade of his nose,
arms wrapped one inside the other.

Or so Sir Henry Raeburn, R.A., did him
in oils, c. 1794.

Those fine cross-hatchings on the Loch
are not from all the Reverend's parishioners
celebrating after service, skating up a storm,
for the hills and the sky seem no less
skated upon.
It's Time. As surely as ice, oils crack.

Nor is the clerical top hat what it was.
You'll find the ghost of its earlier brim,
painted out imperfectly, is aimed low
as if a moment ago the vicar was searching
for a flashy trout.

He has, it appears, raised his sights
to the deepening blue of night, or something
more distant. He dedicates a miracle
to it, no major miracle, mind you, but still . . .

He makes his turn (notice the sliver of ice
kicked up by the heel of a skate),
has all but completed the figure 6
he means to raise
to an 8.

RIDING THE TIRE

The world's a bog. It's been raining, slowly,
grimly, for days. A good many things
have gone under.

If I'm still here as surely as there's life
in the gray-greens on soggy whole-wheat,
it's not my idea.

The radio comes and goes, announcing
lively disasters in foreign parts, and once
a steady, high-pitched whine

is followed by a tornado
alert for Berkshire and Hampshire Counties.
Never my own. All afternoon

I've seen the big blue-blacks
rumble across the north, have seen their
distant firing. I do not think they'll fire on me.

In such a seep
my going on might as well
be proliferation of cultures in a petri dish,

my exit from the softening house
merely an absence
of any refusal to exit.

Without, it's grisly in the east all right,
neither raining nor not.
But westward

how the willows glisten,
all those flashy little leaves like swallows
banking on the sun.

Even the balding tire dangling from the maple
is bright, every last statistic showing.
From its dirt-filled trough

a Black-eyed Susan shines. I can do
no less, climb in, am rounded out. Higher
and higher I ride the tire.

KILLING TIME

Just out of sight of the bridge on Hungary Road
I'm killing time while my grandson casts
for trout too cagey to show their spots
where the water bubbles and eddies below a fall.

Beer glass glitters, a dirt bike mutters. No luck
here, and we move downstream.
Salmon Brook widens and deepens, is overhung
by a sycamore

kids must once have monkeyed up
to the fraying rope still dangling from a limb.
I find a sitting-stone, pull out the May number
of *Poetry*, and presently two damselflies

shift their affair from phlox to the written word.
One has white-spotted jet black wings

and an iridescent blue-green abdomen;
the other is dun but completes the circle begun

when the first gripped her neck with his tail.
She bends a dusky abdomen up to his, strokes
seed from him with delicate and digital concern.
When every so often she pauses, his wings

blur. Clinging to page 86 – oh flagrant delight –
the two are right over Eamon Grennan's
"free of memory and forecast." This is killing
time the way it ought to be,

not the way I counted knots on the swing-rope
a moment ago – like telling beads.
What it's for is climbing, knot by knot, swinging
out, in, out, letting go with a cry, in love

with flying. I feel the cry rise in me –
but no, it's my grandson's. He has hooked,
amazingly, a many-colored Brown
that shimmies over the brook, shimmies and

backflips, is gone. And there the damselflies go
and the dirt bike's back and a tolling of traffic on
Hungary Bridge. What it tells and tells
is time.

THIS

Fresh from the elegant park at Coole
and the Celtic crosses of County Mayo,
more at home in that other world
than here at Scrubby Neck,

I hear them again, close overhead,
see their crossing – the black swans,
necks stretching for the Gay Head cliffs,
wings whistling *this This, this This.*

VI. MORE THAN I AM

INIS MEÁIN

Considering millennia of tooth and bone and carapace
drifting down in a nameless sea to pave
this barren land for boulders rolled by glaciers to inscribe,
considering the generations that hoisted
the scribbling stones to wind-breaking, wind-wailing walls
to story the land, scratched up what little soil welled

in cracks, hauled seaweed, goat dung and pulverized rock
in sally baskets tumped to brows to cover
the old stone text with loam — considering such
revising, I am more than I am who in a minor plot today
plant rhyming rows
of seed potatoes, withered things, and pray
they will translate well, bloom white as tooth and bone.

AFTER WATERLOO, WHAT

he engineered were parapets of dirt
around the perimeter of his empire at Deadwood
to fend off the madding trade winds and the eyes
of the English, so many hundreds
to keep him in his desert enclave on St. Helena.

Inside the parapets he saw to the installation
of a formal garden sufficient to halt the advance
of an enemy more clever than his witless jailors.

When the hundred peach trees of its promenade
wilted, canaries in the aviary and koi in the pool
keeled, and the pièce de résistance, imperial eagle
made of local clay
had the wings of a cormorant hung out to dry,

he had to laugh that charmingly rueful laugh.
The worst was the fountain that sputtered like
an old man's seed. He disappeared for days.

And still —
throughout the summer of 1820 guards saw
the bloated Emperor (no one suspected arsenic)
wielding a watering can at 5 a.m.
in his tattered nightgown and dirty red headband.

Barely able to walk, he persisted
in irrigating his pennyroyals, passion flowers
and seven kinds of rose.

He called the first his Marie-Louises, the second
his Josephines, the rest his Little Ladies.
They would never remarry, carried on no affairs,
told no one of his "difficulty." They were all
the forces he had left

to fight the enemy — not the assassin who laced
his white Bordeaux with arsenic
but the sot who knew the poison by heart
and drank it gladly.

THANKSGIVING, FIN DE SIÈCLE

Her timbers creak like the century
when she pulls herself up from her recliner for reasons
she forgets and shuffles painfully, gripping the arms
of her walker, as once she held — whose arm was it,

she wonders, shuffling from room to room — so many
photographs of men in uniform and ladies in waiting
for them to return, ladies
in veils for grief, for weddings, for reasons she forgets,

and pictures of children, grand and great
grandchildren, all the same. Are they her dream
or she theirs? And where is whatever she left behind
to get wherever she is,

and why is she in the midst of so much
empty space she wishes would shrink, enclose her
like a mahogany box with a ceiling of silk like clouds,
like —

No she doesn't. She takes it back. One foot goes
before the other, and there it is, she remembers now,
the recliner. She has made the circuit.
Thanks be.

FLOWER FARMER

Last fall Mr. Dewey wrapped his house
with sheets of plastic.
Lit by headlights, it glittered red and blue.

This spring it lists farther, the shingles flap,
and you can hear, he says, the tick
of water dripping, termites, beetles, mice.
As for his greenhouse, it's held up by vines
and sprouts patched stovepipes crookedly.
All winter Mr. D "cooked dirt" for potting.

He's out of sorts today.
She's dead, the '57 DeSoto that pumped river
to his flowers. Still, it's spring,
his dentures sparkle,
he's in better shape than that neighbor of his
with the heart thing,

and there's always the granddaughter.
She's a one with glads,
a natural with daffs and 'lips
but a little wild for boys, he's glad to say —
plant her here, she comes up there.

Putting in carnations this morning
he found another arrowhead.
Onyx, an ornamental. He looked it up.

Ask to see his Indian stuff, he'll ask you in.
Old man smell and mildew and dry rot

and catstink and African violets everywhere,
furry as an old man's ears.

He has, he says, the Indians cold –
knives, scrapers, axes, mauls.
He's proudest of a three-foot pestle stone,
the tip worn smooth.
According to the museum man
it was hung from a sapling to pound seeds.

He can see it now. She's something,
the girl who works the pestle stone.
A sapling pulls it up, the maiden pulls it
down, sapling up, maiden down,
grinding lilyroot. The face of her joy
is his granddaughter's face.

Mr. D is bent
like a tree the pestle stone's done with.
But he turns the stone in his hands, in love
with whatever works. Damn DeSoto!

THE INSTITUTION OF SEED

*for the scientists of the Institute of Plant Industry,
Leningrad, 1941-1942*

The long siege began with bombardment. The fire
burning Leningrad turned our smoke-smothered days
blood-red. Breathing came hard. Stone and dirt
blossomed when Nazi shells fell short in the fields

and still we continued to harvest. When one of us
was hit, bits of limb and torso staining the sky,
we made ourselves go on

digging seed potatoes from mounded ridges
too like the raised earth above so many newly dead.
We were that desperate, digging up

pure strains of every known variety, preserving
what our fathers' fathers and theirs for generations
had cultivated —

the long white Strobs, round red Nevskies
and saffron Lugovskies, saved against disasters
worse than war. Replanted every year,
not a strain should be lost, whatever else might be.

All winter, we lost. Shells falling on St. Isaac's
blew out our Institute windows. The mercury
also fell, the winter of '42 the coldest on record.
No wood or coal got through the blockade,

so we burned what we could, floorboards, chairs,
to keep from freezing
the tons of heirloom seed — wheat, corn, rice,
and seed potatoes.

In January, rats invaded. We shifted it all to
ammunition cans, beat back the rats with whatever
hadn't burned. But that other gnawing

of hunger! And the fury of that other beating —
hundreds beating pans beyond our walls, drumming,

drumming for food. What sustained us was belief

in a day more terrible when pure seed would be all
that could save the race, a day we had to hold
up against the accusation of gaunt faces,
bones surfacing like our own.

One morning we found Dimitri Ivanov dead at
his desk, frozen. Cradled between his arms
were dozens of packets of rice, a rare variety
he'd kept from freezing. Not a packet was open.

In early March those of us left
took as much of our stock as we could
by late night runs beneath the strafing Messerschmitts
across the ice of Lake Ladoga to caves in the Urals.

That summer, we knew, a mountain field would
flower cream, yellow, pink with bean, onion, rutabaga
and the bridal white of potato, regenerating.

THE SON

It's quiet out here in the barn. There's time to think
how six hundred acres came to be worth
a quarter what I paid,
soy beans, feed corn rotting in the field,

and how I couldn't see what I was up against –
except Aloysius Hammer, come out from the bank
to say "Sorry, Tom, but no, not this time."

The auctioneer was Jay Kyle, Roy's son.
Three counties showed up.
Someone was selling beer and franks,
and during breathers Ike Kassit played his fiddle
until my brother cracked it.

It wasn't just equipment and stock
but the linen tablecloth, china, loveseat, every stick
we owned, and a piece of Abbie with each.
She wouldn't come near me, hid the boy behind her.
They gave us a week to leave.

As I said, it's quiet out here. The air at least
is slow to rush in, leaves space
where they were – the Deere, the Harvester,
nine hundred pounds of sow, a mowful of timothy.

The cool eye of the Smith & Wesson is a comfort
I hold to my head.

What stops me is column on column
of head marks, white lines by the door to mark us
at ten, twelve, fourteen. We're all there,
my father taller than his, his son beyond him
by a head, my Jim three inches more last year alone.

And this – framed by a hole in the siding,
the headstones on the hill, each looking over those
before it. That much at least belongs to me
and an easement out to tend the graves.
It's time I did.

THE DANCING

After your first chemo we head for the shore
where summer after summer you danced
from Green Hill to Galilee before your fortune
turned to bearing, raising, then this.

At dead low we reach the rock-cobbled mudflat
at Matunuck, discover the mussels have vanished,
even the smallest hacked off by lubbers
from shacks and RV's multiplying extravagantly.

In the heart of late afternoon, we wait out
low tide, give the surf – and surfers, if any
are left – time to ride in where boulders heave
the incoming sea to rip-curls.

And now they come, as ever, with neon boards,
balancing, balancing, riding the crest above
the dark below. What's life without risk?
We concentrate on the art of it.

SUTTEE

In the heat of the pyre, his right hand rose
and curled to a fist he shook at me, as always.
Not long ago, I would have been burned
beside him, and now was expected to burn

more painfully – in decades of shame

I refused. These days I burn otherwise — with a fury
so forbidden my hand shakes even now as I write
how he rewarded

the scantness of my dowry,
took me like a harlot on our wedding night,
smothered my face with the bridal gown,
bruised my throat,

the scream with which he finished
the same I heard from him in the servants' quarters.
Too many of their children
have his jaw.

The ashes still warm, his younger brother took me
to Vrindavan, City of Widows
where women in threadbare saris held out
their pittance bowls as I would not.

I have found my way to serve Krishna
in the Temple of Satyana-ra-yana, dancing for Him
to the beat of the tabla,
the drummer's hands a blur rejoicing my limbs.

I am learning the uses of my self, learning to ring
however many of my hundred ankle bells I wish.

CATHEDRAL FIRE, 1956

When I got there, St. Joseph's was
too far gone to be saved,
a column of smoke from afar

and closer,
a pillar of fire.
Then the rose window blossomed,

exploded.   A whirlwind arose
and from the belfry, bells,
bells ringing their terrible changes.

As the organ fell
from the choir loft to the nave,
the battering, the heat, something

set it chiming,
playing its sharps and flats
in a fugue of its own creation.

May you and I go down
with such an explosion of music,
a song of songs.

for Fran

VII. SMALL LIFE RISING

JOCIE AT ADVENT

She no longer goes out,
lets dust collect, at home with it
like snow settling in the glass globe
she turns this way and that.
    Oh the bright little people within,
    their ageless sleigh, their song.

It is the season
for candles, one in every window.
She lights one for her father,
how little he weighed at the end,
how slight the skin which kept life in.

And one for the Morgan
who steamed like a field in his pride,
went lame, half blind, in the end
was dragged off by a tractor.

And a candle for herself, her dust
as brief as snow in a globe of glass.
    But such bright little people within,
    their ageless sleigh, their song.

She rocks and waits
for the light to flicker, waits
for darkness like the lake she dove
as a child.
    Oh the bright little stones rising
    to greet me, the aggies and cat's-eyes,
    their glimmer in the dark.

TRAINING THE EYES

for Alexandra and Jocie

Walking straight to the river with Alex
on my shoulders, hands reining me,
turning my head, is better
than so much circling of the fact:

Jocie has gone under, will not recover.
We stop where the river turns back
on itself, dangle our feet from the bank,
consider the current.

I watch the confusion
of the surface, a caddis fly fluttering,
then floating like Ophelia.
Alex sees it

otherwise, says the river is a fish.
At first I don't, then do see shadows
of caddis fly and leaf wrack,
magnified, riding the amber river bed:

the spots of an enormous trout.
Now the current slurs
like someone stricken straining to
speak. I listen harder —

to Jocie saying again how her father
took her, newly born,
to the barn to touch the nervous flank
of Sirro the Arab — to live forever.

VALENTINE

for James Merrill, 2.13.95

Almost Saint Valentine's, this bright auspicious day
when the bells of your seaside village toll to say
the Spirits have claimed their most telling
translator. Toll, that is, as you would have them.

How like you, JM (who insisted
on a purple, starred kimono and crimson slippers
for the occasion of your incineration)
to have the bells, like a nuptial heart, beat so quickly,

and to chime in, once removed, so merrily
in your ex's elegy
concerning his latest amorous catastrophe
thus – "My dear boy, have you considered a corgi?"

"Or tulips?" I can hear you add. You loved
it all, and let us in on it. Small wonder
that after your newest beloved,
kissing your ashes, sweeps down the aisle, rushing

you to the softly purring limo, I see at the tip
of my cramp-toed shoe, mundane planchette,
the twinkle of a coin, two bits,
as if in passing you tossed it off, new minted,

the bride's bouquet or a quip to counter mortality.
P.S. Having seen you to your digs, I make my way
down to your harbor, where the swans let loose
like tugs – with whistles. How little, JM, is mute.

SMALL LIFE RISING

for Gladys Egdahl Couch

Left behind, I've followed her
to this windy height in the hills of West Virginia.
Under a rattling canopy
I shiver, listen to the Word, hear praises sung.

Her cherry box is poised on slings above a gape
too like her open mouth those days she lay there
waiting, dark rattle rising in her throat.
I look away.

Overhead, a Red Shoulder riding the wind
is not, of course, what I wish it to be.
A hawk's a hawk, focused
on matters of moment — milk snake, rabbit, vole.

The box sways on its slings, the winch grinding
out of sync with the Twenty-third Psalm, and there
she goes. Dear God, my mind is
slipping.

Let me think — of anything — of the underground
deposit of salt that made this town —
river water superheated to steam, pressured
down through sixty feet of shale to melt the salt,

the brine pumped back (hue of the death collecting
in a dun deposit on her lips)
to evaporating tanks, from which the fine white
salt of West Virginia came. How good to believe

her bones will rise no less, sluff death, and shine
in their dance. But now the box hits bottom bluntly.
I'm brought up short, in time for the dive of the hawk,
the kill, the small life rising, completely loved.

MARK'S AUTO PARTS

In come the wrecks to Mark's
and out the gear knobs, gas tanks,
radiators, speakers, mufflers.
Bins of parts.

The crummiest clunker is worth
Mark's while. There's an alley
of front ends – Beetles, Buicks, Jags,
a '49 Nash,

an avenue of chassis,
a park of gutted bodies piled on
one another like lovers. Everything has
a future.

All of which is very gratifying, a sign
of what we'll amount to
in the after time.

The loosestrife will take this, frogs
that, the earth will value
our humus, the cardinal put us to use.
Dismantled, we'll go far.

VIII. BESTIARY

SKUNK CABBAGE

A rattle of winter-stiff grass in the field
and in the sheep shed, a ewe, mother-mumbling
deep in her throat, speaking to the larger
of two lambs still orange with birth.

The ewe is busy licking him, butting him
toward a teat, paying no attention
to the other in a corner,
giving up.

It's all quite peaceful, this dying.
Already the ewe, as she licks and butts,
is scratching a trough to which to nudge what
didn't work out.

I rub the runt angrily, press his mouth
against a nipple, knead his neck
to start the swallowing,
and force the milk —

too fast. He chokes, eyes bulged,
and from the nose, small bubbles, unbroken.
It's an act. I tell the legs to kick, the eyes
to look lively. They don't, they mean it.

Digging a grave at the edge of the bog,
the muck in love with my shovel, sucking it in,
down I go.
How lovely the dark . . .

And from below, from the hacked roots
of skunk cabbage — that purple, spotted thrust
to come — a sharp sour scent muscles up,
says *Live, God damn you, live!*

WAR STORY

With a foot of spring snow on the ground, more
incoming, I drift off by the wood stove. The thunder
of a town plow beyond the hemlock hedge homes in,

shaking me awake (tanks tearing up Hung Phu Alley,
thin nh walls trembling). I try to forget, slowly
recognize what's half growl, half hum

at the kitchen door — rise to see
a grizzled, rat-tailed, long-nosed good-for-nothing
scavenging the cat's leftovers. I play dead

behind the glass, old bag of bones, and the possum
flexes his fur, looms large as if he's more than himself.
No, I see now, *herself* — big-bellied,

eating for a crowd of pea-sized progeny
guzzling in her fur-lined pouch. Blindly they crawled
the world of her to this nursery

in which to hide until the going's good. I drift off again,
climb into the pouch myself
to wait out war — that purely human crusade.

WINTERING OVER

All winter he does what he can to fend off the cold
with savory apple and birch, tough locust, hickory, oak.
The fire is conversation. Then in the silence of night
a groaning, rattle of windows; she settles more deeply,
her ridgepole sagging. All winter he waits for her

to come alive with otherworldly wings, a stir in the crawl
space above: blunder and whir of paper-making wasps
in March, emerged from dark cells of breathless dream,
flutter of unfurled bats, tapping of a downy on clapboard.
And just like that,

it's mud time, and out from nooks in the fieldstone
cellar, garter snakes ripe with mice swell up and work
their way to the first floor, and again he shares
the pine boards of a warming kitchen with lazing
muscle boys unfurling in snakeskin shafts of sun
or stretching by the baseboard heater.

He sleeps better and wakes to what's on its beat
in the attic, along with the *tick tick tick* of familiars
who slept all winter with him, high up
in all four corners, dark vees of them huddled
for what little warmth they generated,

who now, in the new tilt of the sun, are walking again
the ceiling and wall, climbing window glass,
lifting the seven-spotted red of their beetle backs
to reveal they too have wings to take short flights
over puddles of light – from mullion to pane to sill,

tick, tick, tick.

It's not to fly away home
that they make these puddle-jumping flights, for see
how unlady-like they are, one landing on another, quick
to make more of themselves.

Here, between such stirring wings on high
and such uncoiling below,
he begins again.

VALLEY OF THE NAUGATUCK

After winter's discontent, I love
how you stretch out, rising and falling
as I move deeper into you – lush

scents in the slick of rain redoubled:
wry aromas from last year's leaves,
umber odors from the mud,

sweet from syringa, shadblow, cherry,
lubricious from the musk, discreet,
of a skunk –

love how this scrim of rain
refines flamboyance to the subtle hues
of an Utamaro courtesan,

each washing into each –
how pleat by pleat your hills open
to whitewater muscling darkly

below a who's who of high school love,
tall tales all colors on a bluff,
grown wistful in their veiling by the mist.

SWAMP SONG

This warping of the ordinary,
these weftings of song,
such trills and profundos
threading the night

unravel instantly
as ring-tailed, nimble-handed
managers of margin
fatten on the fringe and have

done
when rain begins to rattle
and raises more
stridently the ruckus of frogs.

Tomorrow the sword-beaked
Blue will hunt them
down. Their death will be
mute

as the stalk of the heron.
But now in the rain-
washed warp of the bog, such
weftings of song.

AS THE WORLD TURNS

*In anatomical terms, the snood is an erectile, fleshy member protruding
from a male turkey's forehead. Most of the time when the turkey is in a
relaxed state, the snood is pale and 2-3 cm. long, but when he begins his
courtship display, the snood engorges with blood, becomes redder and
elongates several centimeters, hanging over the beak and dangling below
it. Female turkeys prefer to mate with long-snooded males.*

How he struts and pauses, turns this way and that,
the better to give her a gander at his pricked up tail,
feathers fanned out like face cards in a royal flush.
When she shows a poker face, he cranks his engine,

a flivver beginning to gobble,
flashes the sheen of side-feathers, beige fenders
hiding the mortal feet he goes upon, neon blue head
tucked close to puffed up pectorals.

He's grown a little Charlie Chan goatee – it dangles
importantly below a red display of wattle. And now
the strange snood swells and droops from his beak.
He swings it side to side. *Behold, my love!*

She does not see and does not see, then carelessly
rises as if *en pointe,* stretches her wings (she has them!),
picks a nit and strolls, oblivious, into the undergrowth.

He fans his tail more winningly, pulls in his head,
expands his sun-struck, medaled chest, and marches
toward her arch of briars.

GETTING RELIGION

Flood's Cove, 1978

And next they're wigwamming
spruce, old pilings, driftwood,
half a lobster pot,
the rotted ladder from the pier,
topping it off with Deb's panties
and one of her bras
for tonight's bonfire.

Before they light up the sky
they clown around
on the roof of the lobster shed,
dive thirty feet
to water just deep enough
to prove their lives are charmed,

then take to dories, work a school,
hook much of it on mackerel trees
and lay it out at the water's edge.
They hack, heave fish heads high
for gulls, leave the guts to crabs.

Now here's a sight. The boys are
silent, hunker on rockweed
to watch a thrashing of the water.

An eel is making mincemeat
of fish guts, crabs, the works.
It's five feet long, thick
as Johnny Thompson's forearm –
enough to give a boy religion.

ROCK BAND WITH FIREFLIES

I am too old. All the more reason to love,
across a field, a flood plain, and a river,
the syncopated cadence of the drums,

ground of the bass, illiterate wail of rock
at the strobe-lit dance of a summer school
on its bluff across the Farmington – love

how the music comes, goes and comes again
in the currents of a cooling night,
how it matches the fireflies sparking

over the smartweed, vetch and ryegrass
of a spring-fed field and among the small
moon-struck willow leaves,

flashing like an amplifier's green golds,
each firefly's strobe a separate code,
each signaling *I Am*

the one, and each one right – like the stars
in that other ceremony overhead,
whose fires flare up and fade and flare again.

How old must one be not to be one
of the ones?

REGATTA

All night beneath the stately turn
of the slooped and schoonered sky,
they rode the star-filled swells

expensively, their halyards chiming,
that now are under jib and spinnaker.
From this hill, this humming top,

it might be ivory queens, bishops,
kings, gowns billowing
who make their cryptic moves

across the mottled bay.
Overhead, a skein of swans,
wings working up the air to whistle,

and this for heraldry —
a blue and silver kite, an osprey,
a redtail rounding out

the sky. How hard to believe
in anything
less heavenly. But there it is,

the dive, direct hit of the hawk
and sudden tangent
to the nest,

that innerspring of rabbit rib,
shrew skin, quail down,
fox fur.

As for the yachts, the swift
white yachts,
how many among us

must be taken, bone and gut,
that these may be
so sleek?

THE DARKENING

The whirring rig makes hay,
moves in on the lively center of the field.
The dog runs circles around what goes under.

And it's done.
A low sun colors the long waves of first-cut
yellow, salmon, orange, amber

before it too goes under.
Between the darkening windrows
the meadow seems to glow from beneath,

and the first fireflies, a single star, all things
which aren't going in
come out.

Walking home, I breathe easier. The dog
examines damp scents . . .
Now a sudden thrashing in the hedgerow

breaks into the road. And freezes.

The dog is the first to move, then the fawn,
but not fast enough —

a rent in its throat darkens. Beyond, a doe
crosses the road in a single neck-out leap.
From the other side, her shrilling

cuts through.
I have no idea how long I stand there.
In the end, the night relents,

the fireflies resume, the stars, the field.
But the rows, the long windrows
are dark as stone.

THE TRACKING

Mercury shrinks to its bulb
and the lake freezes fast
to black ice. I see myself
reflected there,

a long Walleye so slowly
passing through my head
it might be a fixed idea.
Now the stars

begin their glittering,
coy-dogs their yip and yowl.
They would have me
celebrate the Hunger Moon,

old skull in the sky.

And a cry cuts through the coys.
The lake is the white
of a wild eye.

At its heart, dark pupil,
a crippled White-tail
spins, is going nowhere.
The cry echoes from all sides.

In sudden silence, what strikes
is elegant, precise.
The deer
is frozen, seems to know

what the lynx
must do. One slash, she kneels;
a single lunge, her throat
is open.

Her death scream lasts
all night. In the first spill of sun
I trace the tracks
to the cache

I force myself to memorize
ribs broken into, empty cage
of the heart, eyes staring
at me. I enter the dark

evergreens. Where the prints
are far apart, I lope,
where closer, I slow,
where closest, stop,

swivel sharp ears. At noon I see

the lynx, basking on
a boulder, oriental in the languor
of its alert. I fire

in the air and continue
long after it retreats, fire
in fury,
in celebration – I have no idea.

THE TESTING

for Dean

In the yard, owl hooting, hooded
silence, then the scream of a rabbit
rising to the upper story of the night
is neatly canceled . . .

and I wake to a knife at my throat,
dug in at Anzio beneath the glitter
of tracers, a cold hand on my chest
testing the bent of my dog tag,

finding me a friend. White teeth
and a whispered *Buona sera*
split the dark, and like a flare hissing,
Attento! The Kraut, he is everywhere.

From a pine close by, the owl again.
How slight our cover, I think,
and turn to the give of you, my love,
the animal murmur.

BEAST IN THE ATTIC

Today's lesson: *It has rained, it is raining, it will*
rain all spring, in Czech. Fat clouds hunker over
the *domecek* I've bought, uncertain foreigner.
It's time to test the attic for leaks, take stock

in this tile-roofed crawl space to which I climb.
I bend low under the downpour's drubbing,
let my eyes adjust, see something
has been here before me,

something large enough to make a gap
in the southwest corner sufficient to throw light
on brown and black fur,
cairns of scat, some white, some beige or umber.

I go down on all fours, bag in hand, no hurry
under such a pelt of rain. I sniff a knot
of fur, cinnamon-scented, consider the nature
of the beast,

examine the various shades
and twists of its deposits, the earliest hollow
as bird bone, light as chalk, here for decades.
When I look up,

it's there,
long and low as a stoat, ears up, aimed my way,
an ivory bib from chin to legs, too sharp a grin:
a figment no doubt from the earliest place

at the base of my brain.
Still, like someone without papers
at a checkpoint, I back off, leave the attic
to the animal.

THE COLLECTING

for Pablito

1.

First light. We cut engine, drift
to a hull just under the surface. Slow
rings pulse from it, burnished
by the early sun.

Uncle slips a hand through the noose
of the turtle line,
and lowers himself, flex-kneed,
to the Green.

Its head rears up, hissing
as he cinches the neck
and father guns the engine,
drags the turtle too many knots to dive.

I have no choice, haul it in
to my father, who flips it on its back,
slides his hand beneath the carapace
to the elbow, says she's full of eggs

and begins to club her unretracting head
methodically. Her hissing bubbles
through thickening blood
and I spit out like broken teeth
"Enough, enough!"

Even when he carves away the under-shell,
rips out the guts
and throws them to the sharks,
the thudding of her heart continues,

that gourmet treat worth its weight.
But his greatest tenderness is reserved
for the eggs he lifts out one by one.
They'll earn a fortune.

2.

Back in Puerto Angel, the egg-bright moon
almost full, my head against the wall
behind which my father ruts
then snores, I slip into a dark
dream in which I club and club his head.

Enough.
I leave, walk the silver beach,
find tracks four feet apart, away from
and back to the sea,

come on a one-way track
and against the sky a tilting dome.
I crawl so close her labored breath
drowns out the surf,

wait an hour until a bubble
beneath her risen stub of tail slowly
lengthens to the tube
a bulge begins its long way down.
I cup my hand below.

When it drops, warm in my palm, I commit
the egg to memory — cream as a moon,
tough-skinned as old leather.

Already another is on its way.
I gather more than a hundred, spread them
evenly in the hole, and find myself
replacing sand,
matching her own slow swipes with mine.

It's near dawn when she turns and when,
surprising myself, I climb the carapace
I ride precariously, its sway unchanged.
My hands and feet grow raw
from gripping the rim like the edge
of a world.

In the surf I'm washed off easily.

PICKEREL COVE

for David Morse

Past the grassy runways of the local airport
with its buzz of Cessnas, beyond the last wind sock,
below a steep bank littered with junkers
rusting into the earth and pierced by saplings

curls Pickerel Cove, original coil
of the river long since gone straight, backwater home
to all the life the river's too busy to accommodate.

Ease down the bank, uncover the skiff, use a snag
of stricken sycamore for balance, and put in.

There's no hurry. This will take time. You are at first
a sight for all those little periscopes
of lesser painted turtles peering through the scum.
Settle in, be patient, become
a part of it,

wait for the bullfrogs to resume
their song beneath those spires of pickerel weed
and for the long sigh of heron wings overhead,
their soft clap as they're folded in for the stealth
of stilt-legged fishing – a sign you're safe as scenery.

Now it's time to look for a disturbance
of the duckweed – a slow counterclockwise
revolution of quilled algae growing on a two-foot shell
basking just below the surface,
from which a double-fisted, hook-beaked snout

rises, backed by a pair of mud-black eyes
taking you in. Be still, let yourself be known.

Be ready when the snapper sinks slowly,
scrapes the bottom of the boat, raises it like
another world, some Turtle Island,
 and sets you down, different . . .

As you leave, be ready to be lifted again
in deeper water at the bend,
home to the three-foot Imperial Carp

that show themselves just once a year
when two by two they twine, hundreds roiling
the river, their copper, black-bordered scales
enormous, the currency of an ancient culture.
This late in the season, they lie low,

but their surge will swell the surface below you
like the sudden updraft that catches a small plane
unawares, and tosses it, reminder
your welcome here is provisional.

TIME BEING

It's all over. The bony maple
proves it, and the sunflowers, burnt out,
necks broken.

The tree toads think

otherwise. They gossip from limb to limb,
throats bulging ripe as melons.

And that fall-colored stem-strider
exactly yellow and mold-specked enough
to make a bird think *leaf, dead leaf*

is busy basking on a vine,
seizing the Indian day as if it's for good.
Nice way to make a living.

I can't afford it,
go on harvesting potatoes and beets,
digging quickly, building up equity,

nimbly selecting the best of the crop
and heaving the rest of it
over the fence

to the lambs that browse,
oblivious to what's in store beyond
these mole-gnawed sweets.

Now it's nasturtiums, small change
I throw, rusted petals so light they float,
the frames-per-second slowing.

The blossoms land
on the ram, who freezes, seems to think
a single frame's enough.

Oh lord
of toads and dead-leaf bugs, for the time
being, it is. We hold our pose.

IX. GALLERY

IN WYETH

In Wyeth we never see
so see the more
the thunderheads
an old hound points as if
they are fair game,

and do not see
so see too vividly
in pickaxe and shovel
red with clay
at rest against a rotting stump
the old dog's death.

In Wyeth we are not shown
the way a girl who shores herself
on arms like bone
has hauled herself from house
to barn, from barn to field.
We know.

The art is to suggest, not say,
until we see
not precisely the old man's dory
scrubbed and caulked,
its bow line neatly coiled
in the bone-dry loft of a barn,
and not precisely loss
or all that makes loss gain
but something like
all three.

~220~

DIORAMA : a model representing a scene w/ 3D figures

Now you see
the diamondback's spade of a head
rear so pointedly *Snake*
the frog it has in mind *prey*

poses as a lump of clay *camoflouge*
full of hope
the snake won't know it. [And now
you don't]

see more than bright glass eyes, ⟵ *only visible*
a stretch of scales and hide
on cotton, cork and wire.

(Have faith.) If those two saplings
and a stone
seem unreal, they have you fooled

until halfway down a limb
or in the midst of lichen *natural habitats*
they begin again to be pure

fabrication. Come join me here
at the seam between
the one world and the other.

LAST MINUTE

after "Sleigh Ride," Winslow Homer

Look again. There are crows,
slightly darker than the sky,
circling that cliff
and more below in the winterkill
around the slough.
They can barely wait.

Center left, a two-horse sleigh
on the edge of the cliff rounds a bend
too quickly. A shaft of sun
through a rift in the sky
strikes the couple within. In no time
the dark will close on them.

But all that
will have to wait. The scene
is still on its easel, set for the painter
who enters now, biting into a windfall
Mac, his mood much improved.
He adds a dash of red,

small banner —
the lady's scarf expressing the turn
she leans into, insisting
on tea at four, a fire, festivity.
He wishes her well
against the clenching sky, the crows.

FIRST SNOW IN THE GARDEN
OF THE GEISHAS

after "Giant Snowball" (Tosa School, 18th Century)

Slowly, each flake discrete, a calligraph,
the snow descends on Kyoto.
The sky is a scroll,
its characters spelling the many names
of Buddha.

In this garden of the geishas, the snow
on japonica, laurel and stone
is elaborated
by the day's last sun, like the youngest
geisha, adorned for song, for dance

and pleasures more expensive.
Her face, glazed white,
is deftly rouged, kimono tied like a flower,
outlining her nape in red, highlighting
its blush.

In half an hour the paper lanterns will glow,
the plump-breasted plover on each
an invitation to the narrow lane of Pontocho.
Half an hour and the shamisen will sound,
festivities begin. She knows,

but for now walks the garden,
its pattern blurred by the bright disguise
of snow. Beneath a pretty toy bridge
glide pinioned ducks like polished

courtesans in jade and coral and ivory.

As if to bow, she bends down
to roll a seed of snow
until it is fruit, white fruit.
It grows, unveils the grounds of the garden
where half a year ago she was a novice,

drank saki from the triple cup of love,
wore on her ankles the bells
toward which her hair, unbound at night,
fell softly as the graceful sleeves
of her kimono.

The dark descends,
the snow fruit glows, and above it
a full-faced moon glazed white as hers
leaves the world behind. Far off,
a temple bell. And the shamisen sounds.

SERVING GIRL WITH GALLANTS

after "A Woman Drinking with Two Men," Pieter de Hooch

First the checkered black and amber tiles,
then panes of leaded glass, stage right,
are brushed in, allowing Delft's astonishing light
to gild the room. Now it's time

de Hooch brought in the tavern's newest treasure,
a slender young woman in maroon-red skirt,
tight-waisted purple tunic and linen-wimpled curls,
demure as the Virgin over the mantle. Half turned,

her small feet prim on a tile, precariously
she lifts a wine glass and through its prism sees
those slapdash gallants at table, colored in quickly,
to whom she is to sing. The first taps his knee,

the other like a cricket rubs a pair of meerschaums,
winking. Judging by those red-plumed broadbrims
and that orange, white-tasseled sash, they come from
the greater world of the provincial map behind them.

It's lost on them that they too are the usual
pawns, though we at our remove
can see how the chessboard floor shows through
one dandy's handsome pair of oxblood boots.

Upstage, the old serving woman, eyes averted,
who brings a brazier of coals to warm the worldly
assumes her part is to be used. But the girl —
de Hooch has her hold the goblet up uncertainly

as if to shed light on a dark passage. Her Rhenish,
kindling in a shaft of sunlight, trembles.
The painter regrets his part in what's impending
but needs a sale, checkmated as he is by debt.

THE RECTOR'S WIFE

for Elizabeth Rinehart McQuilkin, 1870-1938

How dark it is from the nave to the altar,
how many shades of obsidian, onyx and anthracite
in the black of his robe. And how stark

the white of his collar.

He is giving the sermon.
Behind him, her face a mask the ecru of old lace,
hands sallow as weathered bone, his wife, who once
won the conservatory's Chopin competition,

is at the organ, its keys like serried rows
of sharpened teeth. She believes in Redemption,
visits the sick five days a week, calls altar flowers
a form of temptation.

For the short season of these few lines, let her be
among the roses, glads, and cosmos she was picking,
flush-faced, humming lieder,
when he came up to preach salvation.

after an oil by Robert Marx, title unknown

SHEEP OF PENTECOST

after "Pentecost" by Peter Ralston

At the stern of the *Edwin Drake*, surrounded
by his trawling nets hung with block and tackle,
she has turned away from him, looks back to
the skiff in tow with its cargo

of sheep – ewes with their spring lambs
bumping teat and guzzling
in this chaos of diesel drone and mother bleat.
All those, that is, he spared from Easter slaughter.

She loves the way each lamb knows its mother
by a deep-throated call imprinted on it
in the womb — she has been singing for weeks
low down in herself.

The cresting, foaming ocean might be
the fleece he sheered from the ewes, naked now,
being ferried to their summer grazing ground
on a barren island,

its stone cross marking the spot
where one of his forebears proclaimed *All this
is mine.* On a bluff above, she knows, is the ram,
defying capture every fall for a dozen years.

Horns sharpened on the cross,
ears aimed at the skiff, matted coat shaggy,
gold eyes cocked behind the length of its muzzle,
the ram waits.

In the wheelhouse he rides the sea roughshod,
has entered into a sort of pact with the ram,
she thinks — *ewes to mount mean chops and mutton,*
the flock increasing every year.

She looks back to the steeple in Port Clyde
this day of Pentecost when cloven tongues of fire
inspired the Apostles
and crosses her arms on the swell of her belly

between what rides in her and a man
who takes her as he pleases
like the steel prow of his trawler bucking
the eight-foot waves of Penobscot Bay,

or the ram that is said to have broken ribs
of ewes in heat, gored his young
and lifted a sheepdog on his twisted horns,
tossed it from a cliff to the boulders below.

She imagines the ram caught by the coil
of his horns in a tangle of briars
and slits his upturned throat.

In a fury of love
she sings to what listens in the fullness of her.

SELF-PORTRAITS

Even that docile Mannerist Christofano Allori knew –
he made the bloody head of murderous Holofernes
(held up by Judith at arm's length by a tuft of shaggy hair)
his own.

In Michelangelo's *Last Judgment* in the Sistine Chapel
his huge executioner, skinner's knife in hand, hoisting
the trophy pelt of Saint Bartholomew
like the hide of a kill he might hang in his den,
has the face of Michelangelo.

And Hieronymus Bosch painted himself as the centerpiece
of Hell, his torso a sort of hollow, see-through egg
full of whores and drunks. He looks back at us with such
a familiar face . . .

We're all in this together.
Squinting down the length of my rifle, lining up

crosshairs on the blue-black eye of an eight-foot rat snake
sliding along a white-mottled sycamore branch, homing
on a nestful of rose-breasted fledglings,

I tighten my grip on the cold of the barrel, suspend my
breath, finger squeezing slowly, slowly,
and see the snout of the snake, framed in my sights, become
my own tight lips, the quiet, concentrated knot of my face.

ON ASSIGNMENT IN UGANDA

after a Newsweek *photograph, 4.3.00, by Peter Andrews*

I focus my lens on the boy's upper lip
with its curve and cleft of love's bow
strung with a sweet line of lower lip.

He has turned from the broken wall of
a smoldering church, has taken in what
my camera has shot — hundreds

locked inside, charred
piles of bone sparkling with shards
of stained glass. He knew them.

He holds a sprig of rosemary to
breathe through, sweeten the stench.
It doesn't

keep his lower lip from trembling,
tightening, pulling
away from the bow, beginning

to release a scream. Let it be shrill
enough to shatter the lens
I see through.

BRUEGEL'S PLAYERS

after "The Hunters in the Snow," Pieter Bruegel the Elder

How bleak these three who trudge into town
with just one fox to show for the hunt,
their lean dogs slouching behind, heads down,
man and beast dark against the sepia snow.

Above, a murder of crows waits patiently.
Only one of the houses sends up any smoke:
the people's firewood has been commandeered
for the Spanish garrison, there,

against those ice-blue cliffs. But look, oh see,
says Bruegel, the bliss
of a magpie sheering the verdigris
sky, and far below on the sky-green ice, children

skating – such tiny black ciphers enjoying,
a touch of carmine for scarf, dot of pink for face.
Three of them chase a fourth; a small boy,
bent-kneed, makes a V

of his blades; another hunches down, spins a top.
To one side, hands muffed, a young woman,
thin from starvation, stops
to watch. She commits the scene to memory.

EVICTION

I kick the door open. Like a newsreel's
numbers flashing backward, followed
by the latest from the war zone,
a sudden glare

becomes traffic, a sidewalk, the el.
Small reflection in Eccle the Baker's
window, I'm wearing my White Sox cap
over a flyer's leather flaps,

also several coats, both toy holsters –
all I can take with me.
I aim one finger, thumb cocked,
at everyone staring at the odds

and ends of family – a broken loveseat,
a bureau leaking underwear,
a cracked table covered with maps
flapping in the wind – anywhere

I want to go. A boy is tugged past me
by his mother, she publicly
not looking, he backwards like an owl.
I fire and fire

and something, a mattress,
falls from the third story window,
kicks up a litter of trash – butt ends
and bits of glass.

One end dangles in the gutter.
The ticking is filthy

with stains, some fat with tails, some
curled like grins. His.

I fire at these, at the window,
the sky.
And the sidewalk opens,
old Eccle drags a sack the size of me

to the hole, pushes it in.
Scuttle of clawfeet.
The wind rattles the maps – anywhere
I want to go.

HENRI RAYMOND MARIE DE TOULOUSE-LAUTREC-MONTFA

It wasn't that simple.
Besides *Henri* and *Toulouse* and *Lautrec*
there were those other titles to live up to
and – if you asked Rosa la Rouge
or Madame Poupoule –
some spicy sobriquets as well: *Big Spout,
Corkscrew.*

To begin with: *Henri.*
Communicant with certain birds and trees,
he was a child so beautiful his mother
could have cried – the eyes especially, the eyes
in which his thoughts, like bright fish,
moved just below the surface.

Then *Raymond* – after his uncle the Count

who was trampled while riding to hounds.
It ran in the family. No surprise then
when his namesake fell and broke, grew
no taller than a troll. Frog-lipped, hugely
nosed, he made a virtue of stunted legs,
declared the world to be a circus
and he its dearest freak,
a man the whores would pay to serve.

He'd rise from a night with them
and one or two hours of sleep
to gather his tools, purely *Marie* again
devoted to his copper plates and canvases.

But he never forgot he was a *Toulouse*
whose people had owned the south of France
and the ear of God. He was born to it,
would tell how his mother kept a bevy of nuns
in one of her chateaus, their only duty
to pray for his sins,
which he was therefore obliged to commit.

He was, after hours, *Lautrec* — "low tricks,"
the envious English quipped. He loved
the drunks, the can-can girls, the aging whores,
was so much a part of the brothel where
he paid handsomely for bed, board and studio
he might have been a gilded ceiling mirror.
Mornings, he stole into their rooms
to sketch the bare-faced ladies before they woke.

At the height of his notoriety, syphilitic, suddenly
no one, *Montfa* of Montparnasse no more,
he closed up shop, and suffering from lesions,

painful swelling of the testicles and penis
as well as increasing spasms of hands and feet
and tumors in the brain inducing deafness,

went home.
Curled on the chaise longue at Malromé,
once more *Henri,* he asked for the songs
his mother had reserved for him,
the toy gazelle she'd saved, the silver crucifix.

ST. GREGORY OF THE GOLDEN MOUTH

*Born on Inis Mór in the Aran Islands, sent to Rome in 398. His
coffin is said to have floated to his birthplace in Cill Rónáin. Not
recognized by Rome. He is the subject of a stained glass window
in the small chapel near Synge's Seat on the island of Inis Meáin.*

I was so pretty a pagan the Abbot said he'd have
me sent to Rome – it was a sin the way I cavorted
from crag to crag in uncured sandals
with the fur still bristling on their soles.

I let myself be sent, hating as I did
the stench of burning dung
that hovered like the Aran fog in small stone rooms
and the beat of the terrible rock-breaking waves

on which the brittle black currachs were tossed
like upended beetles, all six oars flailing.
My own father was taken by the breakers
at Bungowla, dashed against the rocks and flayed,

brought home in pieces and puzzled together
by three crones keening like the wind
and warning me to kiss his frozen lips or be going
straight to hell.

His father's bones,
bits of gristle clinging, were dug from their patch
of dirt — old poverty of clay and crumbled stone —
for him to be planted in their place

and soon uprooted for the likes of me. I traded that
for the elegance of Rome, where my golden words
elevated me at the Vatican, the Celtic savage
civilized by velvet robes, at home

with the finest the City could offer,
drinking in the sweet marrow of its osso buco
washed down with papal wine. My new ways came
easily. Something lost must have risen in me

the way sweet-water on the Islands,
siphoned off by limestone swallow holes
to carve out underworlds, would — *mirabile dictu* —
reappear. This lasted thirty years.

I was not prepared, in the midst of Matins,
for that other deeper surging up, like holy wells —
visions of Inis Mór's cursive loop-holed walls
the early sun shone through, embellishing,

and women waiting on the beach at Cill Mhuirbhigh,
circled in mauve or red by their rings of skirt,
and a stone-gray pony backlit on a crag

above Dún Eochla, mane cresting like the surf.

Serving Mass this morning, I saw an open coffin
lengthen to a currach
bearing my gray and glittering remains
to three islands brightly green on a burgundy sea.

RAIN DANCE

Humpbacked with gear, water
gone, legs giving, I stumble
on a coyote lively with maggots.

The buzzards are all
but done. Clack of beak on beak,
a sharpening. They glare, lift wings,
stir sand about me like the aura
of flies about the carcass.

Around another bend, another,
and there in a recess, I see
low on the canyon wall
rust, white and ochre dancers
twelve feet tall,
torsos tapering like arrowheads.

Their heads are skulls,
eyes enormous,
robes ornamented with antelope.
Birds occupy their shoulders.

Beside them, snake spirits rise like
walking sticks or lightning.

A dust devil spinning over scree at
the base of a cliff, a spirit wind full
of sand, settles. The heat returns,

the canyon walls resume
their wavering, and the dancers
repeat their deliberate step.

The drumming of distant thunder
is just the thrum of a hummingbird
hovering by snakeweed.
I find an alcove in which to begin
to be bone, picked clean . . .

and wake to wet wind, the scent
of creosote bush, tall clouds rising
over the rimrock, dark as flint.
Lightning flickers, the rain begins.

Selections from

PRIVATE COLLECTION

ON VIEWING THE DAGUERREOTYPE
"PLAISIR D'HIVER"

May my words display some sense of style
like the sports in this daguerreotype:

what handsome homburgs and bowlers
and oh those waxed or walrus mustachios!

May my words take place on lines as set
as the sturdy runners of the sled

these gents in their brown study sit
upon – hickory rails placed well apart,

a rhyming brace of them curled like prows
baroque enough to make a Viking proud.

And may my words kick up their heels,
let loose their vehicle and send it careening

down the mountain
to dark Hellein or tall Grieskirchen.

ENDANGERED

for William Leverett at eleven

A tiger is in the tree, William says.
Ben says no – tigers are endangered.

But truly there it is – new wings

spread out to dry, black stripes on yellow,
a Tiger Swallowtail.

"This is the bad time — a bird may come,
like crossing North Carefree," William says,

takes out his paints, makes the butterfly
splay on a cloud as white as cotton batting
in a specimen box.

Under it he puts a leafless tree, one limb
barely supporting a swing. At the bottom
by his name he has written *In Dangered*.

ARRANGEMENTS IN BLUE & GOLD

*Whistler's Peacock Room was created in 1876-77 at the
London townhouse of Frederick R. Leyland at about the
same time Whistler was creating his lyrical "nocturnes."*

1. F. R. Leyland, Tycoon

Jeckyll was my decorator, Whistler my painter,
and neither worth a damn.
One crumpled, the other made a mockery of me.

2. Tom Jeckyll, Decorator

And for the walls, Spanish calfskin
hand-tooled with poppies and pomegranates
brought in by Catherine of Aragon.

Outré, quite perfect.

But not for Whistler. "The colours," he said,
scream at my painting."
The popinjay! And Leyland told him to
"touch up the room," then left for Liverpool
to accrue.

So Whistler painted the calfskin
cobalt blue – and over it, floor to ceiling, peacocks,
gold peacocks flaunting!
It might have been Rossetti's backyard, that zoo.

3. Walter Greaves, Painter's Assistant

The day Whistler heard of young Jeckyll's demise
was the usual. He raged
if a ripple marred the azure I applied.
The peacocks he did himself –
jabbed a brush in gold, sparred with the blue,
touché, touché, and strutted the scaffold,

darting his head from side to side,
monocle in and out, the tips of his moustache
quivering like wings. Then down for a view,
hands clasping each other behind him.

"Aren't they marvelous,
the fowl?" he crooned, and did his Jeckyll:
"Oh my room, my beautiful beautiful room,
ruined, quite demolished!"

At four the press arrived,
found him lounging, improving tail feathers
with a brush-tipped pole.

They reported that Jeckyll had gone mad,
painted his bedroom cerulean, gilded
himself, been taken where the walls were soft
enough to keep him from dashing
out his brains, but had managed somehow.

Whistler listened absently,
examined a cuff of his robin's egg suit,
added the yellow kid gloves, the Panama,
the gilt, swan-headed walking stick,
adjusted his lemon cravat,
and thus arranged, flung over his shoulder
"Indeed, that is the effect I seem to have."

4. James McNeill Whistler, Artist

The evening was another matter.
Along the plum-blue Thames, the brick kilns
hissed, their red-gold fires reflecting

infernally, reminding me. The tooled sky
was navy, its constellations parading
like gilt peacocks.

I vowed no more arrangements
in blue and gold, except for variations on
the night. To this I was true, for several days.

UNDER THE SUN

It is warm, unseasonably. Compliant
in the private courtyard of the Emperor
red cyclamen blooms, gaudy
as bent-backed courtiers
before His Most Plenipotent & Provident Majesty,

Rudolf II, who herewith emerges to honor
his blood relation, the Sun. Conveyed in pomp
across the Deer Moat and into the Great Hall
to the cadence of an overture
composed for the occasion, he now holds court

below the gold insignium of Helios on the dome
of his sedan. It is his pleasure to receive lesser lights –
goldsmiths, courtesans, poets, painters
and celebrants of science like Magus Tycho Brahe,
Grand Master of Cosmology,

now approaching His Majesty, obeisance forgotten.
The Magus, who will die soon of a burst bladder
but whose version of the heavens
is all the rage,
arranges himself to deliver an oration.

He declares the Emperor to be Earth
around which the Sun and its entourage turn.
And who must play the Sun
but Magus Tycho Brahe! His nose portends it,
he notes, meaning his stunning proboscis,

prosthesis of gold whose aquiline forebear was

lopped off in a duel. As he turns to face
Arcimboldo's portrait of Rudolf, collation of
fruits and vegetables in which the Imperial nose
is but a ruddy pear,

the only sound is the click of the cosmologist's
jeweled hand on his 24-karat schnoz.
Slowly he begins his ceremonial orbit
of the throne, and direly the Scion of the Sun
rises, brings down his sword on Master Brahe . . .

to dub him.
Stop here, with the Emperor's sense of irony
intact, the Imperial Master of Cosmology sure
of his distinction, no bubbles burst,
no war of religion today.

CLIMBING THE TOWER

Entering at last the poet's Norman tower
I'm met by a clatter of credit card machines.
Mugs and t-shirts.

A push-button brings in Yeats himself
telling of ceremony drowned, rough beasts
on the prowl.

I climb, as archers of William de Burgo
once climbed to shoot Irish peasants
from that embrasure off limits to tourists

where a wing-spread kestrel in its fort of
broken brush is tearing the head off a rat,
punching meat in the maws of its deafening
young. Keep climbing. And there

beyond the dark stone of the winding stair,
a widening circle of sky,
wildflowers rooting in cracks
of the ramparts — blues, citrons, lavenders
that must have given even de Burgo pause
on burnished 13th Century afternoons.

Far off, the seven woods of Coole Park
color in. And below, the Cloon meanders,
reflecting the tower, the rose-purple clouds
and the russet underbelly of a swallow
threading an arch of Butler Bridge.

Now the kestrel from its slot in the tower
splits the sky, blazing device
in the gilding sun — red, blue and buff
rounding into a gyre which tightens
for the kill, but is for now a wild delight.

WHITTLE

He must have taken his time
as I take mine, late day
on this log — such a milling of
cedar chips at my feet,

some thin as shed skin,
some thick where his knife
cut hard, and short or lengthy
as he quickened

or mused on what it was
in the cedar
would come to be.
I'd like to think he thought it

trapped in there
like Ariel in the riven pine —
but of course that's me,
not him.

If now I see gray-blue wings
easing out of a block of wood
like this morning's heron
out of mist, the mist fills in.

I'm left with shavings
and this: whatever our bent,
whatever hate and love may
curl away from you and me,

not even time, which pares us
aimlessly, can tell what shape
our lives will take.

THE KACHINA CARVER

He carves the mountain gods
with their cunning and whimsy, roar
of laughter and anger.

He keeps up with the competition,
takes shortcuts
courtesy of Hobby USA —

its acrylics,
wood burning kit, and Anglo mannikin
he can twist into any position.

But when he's not turning out kachinas
of stunted poplar, legs and arms
glued on for quick sale,

he devotes himself
to those that come from a single
cottonwood root —

down to the very mount on which
the gods are based. At times like these
he and they are of a piece.

GHOST RANCH AMPHITHEATER

In this desert of skulls a shallow bandshell of stone
rises into lavender-clouded turquoise sky –

1000 feet of overhanging red, beige, yellow cliff,
shades of the plastic-flowered, pinwheeled shrines

embellishing the gaudy graveyards of New Mexico.
Such transformation of death to carnival!

Within this empty cowl of stone (memento mori
where echoes congregate) swallows line their nests

with snakeskin, rabbit-brush, and yucca flower –
bowls for generation, cradles for birth.

Selections from

FIRST & LAST

TEN

for Nicole Christianson

Her brother is building the solar system
out of Styrofoam, remote, not talking.
The planets are mostly done, brightly
attached to the sun, the rings of Saturn
in the works on a pasteboard brim.

So she arrays herself in her mother's
abalone shell comb, pink jade earrings,
malachite pendant coiled to strike,
ruby, turquoise, sapphire rings
and cincture of green glass beads.

She jingles into the moonstone night
unsurely, then slowly and faster begins
to spin around herself.

FOR ROSA ROBATA

Auschwitz, 1944

Bone-thin, bald, sixteen, her job
packing gunpowder
in detonators, she steals an ounce

a day for the underground, prays
the sand she sets in its place
will not outweigh what she hides

in the one nitch they don't inspect.
Today, she pushes the black seed in
too quickly.

The bride's sharp pain in her cry
gives her away. Then the stripping,
the ravishing,

the rope slipped on, the scaffold
creaking underfoot – her answer,
her still eyes say, a detonation.

PALEONTOLOGY

for William L.

Scrupulous as a scholar slicing uncut pages
of a first edition, my grandson pares sheaves
of brittle slate.

He looks into the imprint of a Paleozoic fern
and leaning closer, finds
a stalled bee, legs curled, resting for its next foray.

"Nothing's ever lost," he tells me, too intent
to hear the growl and snarl
of hell-bent Harleys

on a speedway below the height
where he works. Watching him parse the old
inscriptions, I pray he's right.

DOING TIME AT GILEAD REGIONAL

I make my way through a wreck
of words, past Arabel and Tony
making out in the corner
of English 3H,
into the hall, where Miss Blum,
the principal, has collared a girl.

Forget it. I hit the road.
Nice country here in E. Gilead
and spring to boot. Cows.
Sun on the run-off,
boulders like Dorsets,
Dorsets like boulders, geese
in the cornfield. Nice all right.

Except for these cabanas
where shackled calves do time
the better to be tender veal,
reminding me

how after class Miss Blum
collared that girl late from Art,
running a corridor, bearing
her latest project.

Out here in E. Gilead the cows
are lowing to no avail – the calves
are at the end of their ropes.
And I, strapped in, no headroom
in my Civic, am just thinking

how the principal collared
that girl with the panoramic

Easter eggs, lifted one, looked
through its sugared window,
saw the tiny figures within
and smiled so benignly

I fancied
the little people came and went
at will, their walls the world,
their case a precedent
for all of us — until the buzzer
sounded. Time for history.

For her offense the girl must do
time, tether her lavish spirit.

THE SILENCE

for Bix Beiderbecke, 1901-1927

Daisy Ellington held her son she called the Duke
to be a genius. He owed it to her
to become one.

Bismark Beiderbecke didn't hold his Bix
to be anything, stuffed his recordings, unopened,
in a closet.

In the end Bix went to his room in Queens
where he persevered night & day, directing fifths
of Jim Beam, bottoms up,

at a cornice, swinging the bottles
from side to side in some Birdland of the mind —
cornets so muted he died of the silence.

THE DEALER

Where neon announces
Flamingo Hilton, Hilton, Hilton
she deals exquisitely, says little.
What's it to her if you lose?
She's the house. Except sometimes

when a jackpot's splatter of coin
is goat's milk in an empty pail
and her fingers,
smart as whips with a double deck,
forget the deal, feel only the squeeze,
release and squeeze of a teat,

she's ten and no one's property.
It's dawn on the ridge
with the eggs to collect.
If she sneaks one, sucks the yolk,
no one will be the wiser, no one
will count the chips,

and whatever clouds loom
are what a child can make of them,
never puffed up, whey-faced
supervisors staring down from
ceiling mirrors, corner mirrors,
catwalks everywhere.

AT THE BAR

for N.S.

Two Jack Daniels, neat,
and I'm less defunct, teeth
my own, kidneys a miracle.
It's time

to tell about the farm,
how my father glittered
as he stuck the dog-eared sow
a friend and I held down.
When her thrashing's a shudder,
two short kicks, a final thrust,

my story falters and I order
another round.

My father can scrub the hog
all he likes, can quarter
until she's merely ham to hang
in a smoke house made
cleverly of crates —

my heart's no longer in it.
I stare at my hands, veins
standing out as black a blue
as the throat of the hog
hung up, head down, to drain.

THE STEAM, THE STEAM

Oh the steam there was back then —
a steam in August from Egdahl's icehouse
where chunks of winter sweltered,

and from the Empire State just in, Track 3,
a steam that hissed through silver wheels
to fill me happily with fear.

There was sweet steam from manure,
sour smoke from piles of leaves
that smoldered damply all November,

and winter mornings from fermenting mash
for the boozing cows — the steam,
the steam.

What's left is a diesel's exhaust
where I idle today, waiting for the light
at 4 & 10 in Farmington. And now a child

on her way to school in the car just ahead
leans out, looks back, and fabricates
fantastic ghosts with her frozen breath.

I crank my window, enter into competition.
Oh the steam, the steam.

FIRST & LAST

From her hospital bed she squints
at her great grandson —
unborn blips on the TV screen.

Skin taut, translucent,
mouth a dry well,
she sees him —

the quick heart's dark bubbling,
bright little links of spine
supple

as fish bone,
a black and white skull to which
she nods hello.

REVISION

for Sylvia Davis

A hard sleet rattles the sash
by which she naps,
strapped into a wheelchair.
What occupies her

is not weather, not where she is,
sixteen, painting and painting

St. Paul de Vence. This evening
the town's *chasseur du lapins*

throws pebbles at her window.
"Viens, viens!" From the cote
of the bell tower, the stroke
of the clapper startles a flock

of pigeons. They whirl
out and shine as she will.
Now, under a waxing moon
such sweet commotion

of corduroy on cotton
and buttons unbuttoned
she cannot hear the crisp
entry of an aid with dinner.

Selections from

GETTING RELIGION

LOVE IN A TIME OF EMPIRE

In the waning days of the empire, we wait
for the enemy to strike, if not today
tomorrow or tomorrow. All is deficit:

the government broke, the army stretched
beyond its means, my son-in-law playing
the field, my daughter forlorn.

So we've gone – my lovely, her children
and I (what else is there to do?) –
fishing

for perch in the pond of my villa-in-ruins.
We wait for them to strike.
Then the boy is screaming and all of us

are dancing like
the four-inch perch cavorting on his hook.
When he and I pose with the fish,

we grin, one of us in love with sport,
the other with irony.
Still, love is love and today is still today.

THE DANCE OF CHARLEY LITTLE BEAR

You never know.
Consider Charley Little Bear
whose only job was drawing his welfare
from how many cities

turning his blood (ten bucks a pint) to booze
and riding the rails with the rest of us.

Small chance
he'd do anything else
until that dawn the ripening sun turned
harrowed fields to gold
against the black of thunderheads
and stalks of lightning
in the west

and he worked himself up to the roof
of a rocking cattle car
an hour out of Wichita
and facing the storm went at a dance
as humped as seed breaking through —

a low and rising dance
on the back of a highballing cattle car
with now and then a whoop
and a leap so high he landed far
beyond the rolling place he'd risen from.

LONG EXPOSURE

for Dick Davis

The end of the year blurs and flickers,
an old film, silent black-and-white.
But this evening a west corner of the sky
is still lit as if with strips of colored paper

some child has cut up
and the moon is heaven's brightest pupil,
a star above it for good attendance,
all very elementary.

I'm walking the dog, talking Dog with him,
when I come upon my neighbor
so unpredictably there's no time to shift
from Dog. For his part, my neighbor's
singing the moon, how high it is, how blue.

The moon glows, the dog points, knows
he's in the picture. My neighbor and I
are in it too, one of those long exposures
where nothing moves.

DEAR BROTHER

for Jock

After the misunderstanding, the harsh words and
breaking up, why try to revive
our brotherhood? We have little in common:
you the high flyer, getter and spender of millions,
religiously alcoholic, obsessively recovered, extreme
in all your loves and hates,

and I your nominal brother, a scribbler straining
to make sense, resigned to the separation
we have perfected, and in the underworld of dream,
preoccupied with reunion. In tonight's resort
the floors, walls, doors and dome are glass.

In order to extend our stay, each of us must
drive a golf ball over a crystal wall hundreds of yards
down lobby. You first, your swing a beauty. The ball
floats over easily. I'll never.

But you place yourself squarely behind me,
mold your shoulders, hips and legs to mine, place
your interlocked hands on my hands, help me begin
the swing. I am poised at the top, arms cocked,
when play is called. I am waiting for it to resume.

VISION

I dream the barn burns,
the animals scream.
I'm to blame.

Next day I slide my hand
in bales
to test for smoldering.

In the thick
of the hay, I find a thing
I mowed last fall,

flat out. Blank eyes
cross-haired with rye
have me in their sights.

SNAKE

And now this knot
of snakes
tangling by the back door,

this writhe of white under-
parts, black uppers, tongues
flicking like switchblades.

The knot rolls, gathers speed,
caroms off the stone wall,
disappears under the spruce.

Next day a snake
is in a basketful of *Gourmets,*
sinuous as wicker,

another coiled
like a root in the ficus pot.
When I pull on a boot,

it's already occupied.
I hurl the snake at a wall.
It leaves a red imprint

intricate
as some Arabic script —
and drops.

No good will come of it,
I know in the knot
at the top of my spine.

And yes, in the night
the wind rises,
an oak splinters the roof,

slate shingles
crackle underfoot.
Overhead, sharp with jags

of rafter and ridgepole,
the opening could swallow
something many times its size.

I stare
into the throat,
black gullet of Heaven.

ST. COLUMCILLE AND THE TOAD

This business of Christianizing
is not for the meek of spirit,
says His Excellence, in light
of the drubbing he gave today

to some spear-happy Picts.
Now by a sweet-flowing burn
in Glen Nevis, naked as Adam
and cleansed by his immersion,

he lets go. When he wakes

he's face to face with the curl
of a rowan leaf
covered with warts from a blight

until it blinks an eye
and swells its pale white throat
like the goitered, good-natured,
unwarlike abbot of Iona.

The toad's gold eye
pulls His Excellence in
to the sun-struck summer lake
he dove as a boy in Donegal,

down through the blood-warm
surface — to the white-pebbled
bottom, with its silver glimmer
of cool waters welling.

It is all too otherworldly
for him. Better the Crusade
he rises to, wild for air.
He thanks God

for his recovery
and boots the toad, suits up in
the cowl of salvation
and reaches for his shillelagh.

DREAM BEAR

I make for the Story Stone —
old totem telling the whereabouts
of The People — reach the bluff

trailhead, look down
on the winding of Frijoles Creek,
trace its distant blaze of cottonwoods
gold against an early snow.

Surprised by blunt bootprints,
I follow them into the darkening firs,
am well down trail

when the prints come clean in shade,
narrow as the heels of axeheads
splaying to sharp toe marks. I've come
this far, am downwind, go on.

Fur bristles now on the trunk
of a Douglas. Claw-sign higher up.
Still, the tracks are close together —
the bear's in no hurry, well fed.

At the bottom, a demolished marker,
illegible, reports whose place this is.
Crisscrossing the creek,
I pick up the pace. After noon,

snow begins. I pass a cellar hole,
take my eye

off the trail, wrench an ankle.

In soft tuff above the Frijoles, I see
caves, haul myself to the closest
none too soon – the snow is turning

to sleet. I kindle a fire,
pillow myself on leaves, stretch out
and play my fingers sleepily
over a backbone

of stone, drift off, dream
I know the acrid tang of canyon oak,
sour musk of cottonwood, ginger
of sycamore,

am at home
with the V's of the creek purling, each
in its separate key.
In the dark of dream, a black shamble . . .

I wake to hear at the cave's mouth
the guttural thing I've been expecting,
pull from the fire the butt end
of a brand,

emerge on all fours,
rise higher than myself, wave the torch,
am rank as the standing bear

whose eyes I see myself reflected in.
I hurl the torch
and smell the bright stink of burnt fur.

The uproar of what I hear
far down the talus is also close by,
is mine.

When I rekindle the fire, unsure
what's dream, what's not,
I find an ochre handprint on the wall,
familiar sign to which I fit my own.

CONFESSION

for Norah Pollard

It will not come out, is displaced in her home,
having lived forever in a walk-up
rich with rodents, silverfish, rotting fruit
and a master like an indoor cat who slept much,
seldom went out, then only to buy oblivion.

Her place is too clean and poor in smells,
she knows, and tells the cat, sits lotus-limbed
by the closet, croons *Lilybeet, Lilybeet, Lilybeet*
and mouths philosophy – how all's for the best,
how cats must adapt.

To calm Lilybeet, she talks nonsense,
limericks, lines from Betjman, Yeats, admits
a lesser sin or two, then more, the worst,
and hears, from high in the closet, absolution
like an engine, cranky at first, then purring.

KILLDEER

Friendship, Maine

Mo Cushing is remembered here
by otherworldly plastic flowers,
also a metallic Monarch on a stake

and a vigil candle so well housed
its flame perseveres in the wind
which turns the model windmill

right over Mo's chest.
Such goings on. It's enough for him
to take heart.

But even if all this Mardi Gras
leaves him cold, he has digs in me
where the dead hide out, waiting

like the sudden gray and umber
white-barred killdeer rising up
beside Mo's stone, wing-dragging,

leading me
deeper into this garden of the dead.

BITTERSWEET

on Three King's Day

The 12th day of Christmas
I traveled a field of snow,
a myriad red stars strewn

on it, gold cases still
clinging to some, enough
to enrich field mice —

a miraculous birth of
berries, hard candy hanging
all fall, now soft and ripe

under foot (three seeds
at the heart of each) —
gifts from above

to tempt the tongue,
bless the small life, allow it
another season.

LAIR OF THE WORD

Paula Toxotius, later canonized, funded a monastery in
Bethlehem for St. Jerome, where he composed many works
including the Vulgate Bible and a panegyric on virginity.

Neither of us was a saint. I was incompletely
married, he fresh from his cave in the desert,
a Vatican scribe by day, by night a Bedouin
hunting his lost lion in the best boudoirs of Rome.

For a small man he had an enormous voice
we ladies vied to hear
vibrate in us, a voice he'd learned from his lion
or so he said. Oh, his stories –

how he heard the lion's orphaned mew, raised her
on rabbit kill, loved her throaty rumbling,
his free hand turning it to Scripture,
Psalms and Acts,

lay with her for warmth through desert nights
and as she reached full size next spring, rode her,
one hand gripping her pelt, the other drawing
inspiration from the sky she raced beneath,

until one evening when he sang her in from
the widening circles she'd taken to, she failed
to appear. He told how he saw her only once
thereafter, etched against the sunset on a height.
There was, he said, nothing

but to return to Antioch, then Constantinople
and Rome, where now he tries to hear her in us
and in his own cries, as far from the known world

as flagrant delighting will go. Which is, I think,
not far enough, not the wilderness
I will him to, the desert where Scripture stalks,
that outland of savage virginity, lair of the Word.

Selections from

PASSAGE

BLACK ICE

First ice on the lake.
Sounds carry like skipping-stones:
the squeak of distant skates,
tags on a dog by the opposite shore.

Through ice so clear
it's the color of lake, I see what
summer obscured: — *change*
trout, all facing one way.

Somewhere below, dug into mud,
turtles — small continents —
are dreaming up another spring.

elder
And you, father, have grown so other-
worldly, the skin of your present
so transparent

you allow us to see
clean through to the kingdom
of your childhood — it holds

against the current.
And deeper down in you is what
knows a stone can skip forever

if it's flat enough
and the wrist is cocked just so —

what knows a death
is the skip that keeps us going.

RESCUE

Driving home to pull my father out
of his oblivion, I go off the road,
carom steeply,
miss an abutment by inches.

While a wrecker digs in and pulls
I hear I'm a lucky guy.
I know, but not just yet. Give me time.
All the way to Dox's Garage, Dox doesn't.

Could be worse, he says, and shows me
a Dodge full of glass,
the soggy char of seats, the remains
of a shoe. Some body work's all I need,

he says. The red sun, sinking, means
delight, says Henry,
who comes for me, full of society.
I see only an abutment.

Home, my father has no idea
who I am. What he's staring at is
beyond me. I have nothing
to say, just hold him and hold him.

GOING UNDER

He no longer cares
for himself. I undress him,
strip down, lead him into

this sort of confessional,

adjust the spray.
Marble legs, blue veined,
amethyst penis too small,
brown coral on his back.

Clearly not my father,
something from the bottom
discovered by a boy
diving for drachmas.
I won't have it.

I lather him, scrub his back,
then more gently
his buttocks, between his legs,
the calves, the shins.

With a grinding of bone
on bone, he lifts an arm,
begins his song. I understand
nothing, not a word I sing,
repeating after him.

COMPANY

He squints at me.
— *What company are you with, young man?*
— *I'm not, daddy, I'm writing a book,*
I'm my own company.
—*Yes, of course, I have a son does that.*

When I try to lead him from the corner
where he has propped himself, he digs in,
has forgotten how to walk.

In the hall my brother smiles sadly
from his other world of T'ai Chi,
wheeling an arm as if something wants up
through the soles of his feet.

I work my father's arms like an old
nutcracker's, and he raises
first one foot then the other onto mine.
I count cadence and *hay foot, straw foot*
march him counterclockwise.

Go to your left your right your left
past Michael's windmill, *Left o-blique*
at the living room, and he's on his own
two feet,

and lord how we
sound off 1-2, sound off 3-4, harmonizing
I know a girl who'll shine your shoe.
She says she don't but I know she do.

The china rattles, the glassware chimes,
and Michael's arm goes
round and round. Whoever he is,
whoever I am, whoever this man saluting
left and right,
we are for now a company.

IN TOUCH

Among bullhead lilies after your box slid into the fire,
father, I ship oars, settle deeper in the skiff,
duckweed filling in my wake.
I doze, then see through half-closed eyes the outline
of an enormous turtle just under the surface.

I run my oar over the shell, gently scrape algae,
and sleepily it circles counterclockwise,
the long neck, ropy as an old man's, slowly lifting
the hooked snout, cocked jaw
my way. Like yours, father, point blank at the end,

all pretense forgotten.
The turtle stares, blinks once, stares
longer, then rests its head on the blood-war m water.
Now, as when I touched your palm-up hand,
half expecting it to turn on mine, slap sense

into me, I tender an oar to the snake-flat head, sedate
and smooth as old leather,
scratch it lightly. It moves slowly from side to side.
And you, father, how your hand trembled under mine –
no sudden snap but a soft closing, final farewell.

BIRTHDAY AT THE
MOTOR VEHICLE DEPT.

In line to be renewed
I inch toward the counter,
deep in my separate dark.

At intervals, a flash.

I am called up, hand over
my self,
sit for a new one, become
the small ID I'm handed,

still warm, but cooling.
The face is beyond me,
distorted as if under water,
and surfaces —

my father's, propped up
by pillows
to keep him from drowning.
His breath slogs,

stops.
And slogs again.
I dampen his cracked mouth,
change the compress

on his brow, take the heat.
He tries to clear the death
from his throat. It rises,
his eyes go higher than I

can follow,
his colors fade to beige,
then ivory.
I smooth out his face,

trace his softened lips,
his nose, unflared,

and cover his eyes.
His warmth has passed

to me, old relay. I'm left
with this license — my name,
birth date, and the red
pronouncement: *Donor.*

YOUR THINGS

I'm feeling small, father,
going through things you won't be needing,
like these jade and ivory kings and bishops
you played to win

and did, the way you always won, even
as a kid. No one's baseball cards stood up
to the Cobbs and Goslins you pitched
at their heads.

And here, a bag of marbles.
Your aggies went *ba bam*, didn't they?
I know. Whenever I missed a trick
your eyes would roll at me, dead on,

knock me out of the game.
For days you'd carry me in your pocket,
polishing.
Next time I'd be sure-fire.

I'll never shake you. Your smell
is in these size thirteens

and three-piece herringbones
I tried to clown in, hating the smell,
the press of it,

like the closet full of you
I hid in, hating
how you gripped my hand to make a boy
a man, how you hugged the air from me. I —

Father, I'd risk my finger bones, my ribs,
and all the rest
if the pile of coats and pants I hold
like you
would have a go at me.

DISCOVERY

In a photo of my parents courting at Oxford,
the sun illuminates my handsome father, casts the bulk
of his shadow over my mother, who all but disappears.
Which is how it was when I came into the picture.

Only years later, after his brilliant image dimmed,
could I see more clearly. How can I say this? Consider
the Villa of the Lost Papyri in Herculaneum,

its fountains, arcades, mosaics, and stunning collection
of marble nudes and obsidian busts with ivory eyes.
When archaeologists, having unearthed such treasure,
descended into dark cellar archives to look for more,

they puzzled over hundreds of cylinders blue-black as coal,
burned some against the cold, kept hunting
until one day someone noticed characters inscribed on
the char of the cylinders. As they were unraveled, a trove

of lost philosophy, drama, and poetry emerged
on brittle papyrus preserved by ash from Vesuvius,
the true treasure. Just so, my mother. An illumination.

ALZHEIMER'S

Movers are carrying out
the last things. From the hearth
he watches

vacantly — like the stripped walls
with their faint outlines of
paintings and mirrors.

Nothing's left but the heirloom
clock she'll soon
take down, shroud in blankets.

She winds it, nudges
the pendulum. In the hollow
house, it echoes loudly.

THE LIGHTERS

In her eighty-ninth year she's reducing
her inventory – china to the children, mementos
to the trash – but in her boudoir
keeps half a dozen square-shouldered Zippos,

on one her husband's initials,
the best man's on another, the rest anyone's guess.
Dry-chambered, their rusted spark wheels stalled,
they are lined up gravely on a jewelry chest

full of antique gap-toothed keys with elaborate
scrollwork on their hilts, fit to open
high-backed steamer trunks, perhaps the door
to a sunken garden

where every night the dry-bones come
in mothballed flannels and hand-knit sweaters
to roll their own, light up
like fireflies and, sotto voce, sing to her.

INVITATION

Mother has shown me the secret
bowl of twigs and twine,
snake skin, horse hair and rabbit fur
in forsythia
trimmed like a hood.

From here, waxwings,
expecting, sang all April
their yellow, tawny, crested songs.
They were mistaken.
They left.

She's careful to leave a gap
in the forsythia for their return
and in herself another for whoever
she was back then, flying through
childhood. In my favorite picture

she's skating, 15, polka dot clown suit
billowing, huge ruffles at the neck,
one leg flat out like a tail, arms
winging for balance, head cocked
to sing. That girl is welcome anytime.

COMET-WATCHING IN THE PITTSFORD CEMETERY

Easter Sunday, 1997

Meal worms have had a field day
in her spices and cereals. When I find
the winged things they've become
are too quick to catch, she's not surprised.

They're angels, she quips, and may half
believe, so many loves have gone under.
Her world's increasingly peopled

with them. Today she planted a totem

blackbird, beak upright with song,
by her husband's tall stone which doubles
as her own, just one of the four dates
still open. At dusk she leads me there –

hill city glowing under a waxing moon –
to see the brightest comet of the century,
twin-tailed and lucid as a Luna,
powder the sky with the stuff we are of.

AUTUMNAL

Here at the edge
of the marsh, pods splitting,

the complicated plaid of her life
unraveling,

she looks to the sky, is happily
a steep-necked bittern imitating

cattail and thistle.
Her spirit-seed is ready to be

on its way
up, and the body-chaff down

to the umber generation of
the under world.

GET USED TO ENDINGS

she says, undone by another,
shuffling down the dust-
hung lane past the old scrub oaks.

She goes slowly,
stops often for breath, too much
a part of this décor

to worry a towhee rustling up grubs
or an osprey on a roadside pole
webbing a wattled nest with fishnet.

She commits it all
to memory, happy to be here to see
again a black swan whistling over

so low she's stirred by the wind
of its wings. Three beats, it's gone,
and she too, soon, into the scenery.

COASTING

Mother — still hale if frailer
at year's end, housebound
for her ninetieth Advent,
two feet of snow

already down,
the house lights flickering —
laughs to see
through thin panes

what rides out the blizzard:
an oak leaf,
brown, sere, curled edges up,
coasting the crust.

LUMINATION

The stories my mother and I tell
on each other at this festival of light
are only harmless

to others at the table.
Now she leans unsteadily to
blow out candles held by clay angels

and her fine white hair catches fire.
It blazes, illuminating the terrified
naughts of her eyes and mouth.

Later, still smelling burnt hair
on these hands that put out the fire
with a fierce laying on,

I think how soon her hair
will again be the first of her

to burn, this time beyond my reach.

I've lost
interest in the stories I tell.
My hands know better.

SHE SEES
FROM HER CRIB BED

three horses
in the year's first snow.
The Palomino flirts,

head over shoulder, rump
to the Bay, leads him
a merry chase.

The White
is another matter,
keeps his distance,

faces down the elements,
so much a part of them
he might be limestone

cropped up from below.
Now, in the come and go
of morning fog, she sees him

float, hollow-boned, wing-
shouldered. There's nowhere
he won't take her.

NURSING

Christmas Eve, 2003

Mother's arms around my neck, I step
backward, lead her from commode to bed,
a half dozen painful steps to each of mine,

an oxygen tube to breathe through
trailing behind umbilically.
I bathe every part of her, never as close

since my other nursing. Later,
attending in the dim light of an Advent
candle, immersed

in the two-beat time of her "breathing tank,"
its pulse my own in the blood-warm dark,
I float in a waterworld where birth is all.

TEA CEREMONY

She has given up eating.
She drinks no more
than a sip of crushed ice.
But how she savors
a bag of smoky Lapsang.
All of her 95 years are
in the bag.

HOLDING

She's talks of journeys
and now this *passage*
as she calls it.
I'm wishing her
bon voyage
bon voyage . . .

but she pauses to tell
another story:
of being on board
a ship just underway
and throwing out a bright
streamer of crepe paper

to someone she loves
on the pier.
The crepe stretches thin
but holds a moment, holds.

She touches my hand,
and I remember her verse:
I will not be homesick
in that strange city . . .
it's the day before I leave
that gets me down,
that other journeying from
room to room.

THE CANE

Knotty, brass-collared, its bone handle
grooved like wrinkled skin,
the eye of a heron at its crook,

her father's cane went everywhere
with her. When airport security
suspected its hickory, beginning to split,

hid contraband,
she shook it, feigned senility,
prevailed.

The less she trusted her pins
the more she trusted the cane to keep her
from a walker or, God help her, wheels.

With it she strode the fairway
of her kitchen, hip-
swinging like her favorite linkster,

and when she took to bed for
good, she kept it close,
would need its support on her journey,

kissed its ivory beak, got a grip on it below
the covers, and when she let go at last,
would not let go of it.

WALK

1.

When it was over, all I could think to do
(no, not think) was clear the walk
while I waited for them to zip you in,
carry you out. I shoveled hard, broke up ice

beneath the cold-white
high-prowed boat of a crescent moon,
a single star in the hold. "This is my birth
day," you'd said, who were now underway.

2.

Before I am prepared
it's spring, your cherry blossoms
fallen thickly.
I brush them off the walk,

see myself sweeping a tea garden
the morning after rain and wind
have tossed the trees.
Whose dream is this I am in?

In the wake of flowerfall
you must have swept just so. I walk
your walk.

CIRCUITRY

The night
of her passage, I listened

to the whole house
listening.
That damned buzzing

in the hall, a faulty connection
all those weeks,
had stopped. And there —

her favorite clock
ticked, as it hadn't for days
since she stopped winding —

the one that kept her
company at night, chiming in
every half hour.

Naturally, just then it did.
Next day no one would admit
to having a hand in it.

I'm not a believer. All I know
is we wanted her back
that badly.

THE LAUNCHING

Please dears, celebrate —
Today is my birth day.
No hearse: a van, bells on,
selling Good Humor.
I am not where I am

supposed to be. Imagine
a balloon: wicker cockpit,
silk shroud laid out,
memento mori
in the early ground fog,

and then with a hiss
it's blossoming
all colors, going going
in the mist, but
before it's gone for good

it shines through a rift.
Just so, I'm here — no,
here. I'm waving,
a launching, a cause for
whistling and applause.

FIGURE GROUND

From the bleached rack
and mud-brown carcass, half-swamped,
of a buck,
a feast for all that goes on in the bog,

I look away
to the hill house
where only two months ago you
looked out from the rise of your hospital bed

and lower my head, notice
the purple hooded twists of stiff skunk cabbage
melting snow between the antlers,
sweet visceral stink

enticing the first fruit flies.
How thin the wall between death and life —
between you
breathing what little you could

and the two of us
in the dark of the adjoining room, unable
to help or sleep, urged on
by the purpling upsurge of our need

for death to be undone. If you heard us at all,
you were not shocked,
for whom life was always a matter
of life and death.

ANOTHER DAY

Please sit for me again, my love,
just beyond the Nepalese prayer flags
and the heirloom clock, not stopped –

sit in your father's salmon pink chair,
cockeyed with gratitude
for whatever it is you are reading,

perhaps the story of Shackleton's endurance
or *Sailing Alone Around the Room*.
Retell the stories, show vistas of the night:

the heavenly party attended by so many
dead friends wearing jeweled masks,
gaudy fingernails painted gold and pink,

and describe again today's dawn-view.
I'd see more clearly the lacquered sun riding
the ridge, another day for you to celebrate.

Please sit for me, Mother. I want more
than the celluloid windows I look through
in this album, wanting in.

GROUNDHOG DAY

Such sun off a glaze of ice, the sort of sheen
you liked, and would all the more so on a day
you loved. I want a sign, just the shade
of one, but you lie low. The season of grief

is long. A red bole of mercury lopped off at zero
is all, and above it the sad drone of a single-engine
plane. Now a metallic shiver
(shades of your teacup trembling happily)

from your country-girl gift to me, tin circus act
propped on the mantle: a tin Cow holding a Ewe
holding a Hog holding a Duck holding a Rooster
crowing – such a tintinnabulation.

It's short-lived, this concatenation, a matter
of frequency, only one tremor in touch
with another, but my belief in emptiness is shaken.

FLY-OVER

I don't know what the black swans do
or where they go, only know how they pass,
how I hear them far off, coming in low
over the dunes, no noisy honking like geese

but a whip-whistling
of wings, not slow like herons but quick,
quick, and there they'll be,

working the ocean air like dolphins, undulating
the long muscles of serpentine neck and
ebony fuselage, the water-raking feet pulled in,
heading back at dusk through the low red sun.

There, mother, I've made the swans the way
you liked them, and now I'm waiting for them
as you and I waited before you too went where

I don't know.

How short and long a time ago we were
together here where I watch in a blind of sorts.
Now – quick, quick – they're coming, but only
one – and that one white. White. And gone.

MY LAB BELIEVES

in more than meets her eyes
in the scrub oaks

we walk through
for the first time without you.

The prints are here, still wet,
delicious, discreetly cloven.

The dog lifts her nose
to get wind of what she's sure

is lying low – just there –
or there –

what looks out carefully,
completely

interested, and will not show –
not ever – except

now and then at night a quick
white flash just vanishing.

LORD GOD BIRD

local name for the Ivory-billed Woodpecker

When I heard the news, mother, I wanted to
call to make it real, hear you yelp
when I told you *The Lord God Bird is back,*
not extinct after all, forgetting, as ever, that you are.
Extinct, that is.

I'm always brought up short by the news.
How? There was so much of you – like the Ivory-billed
that wouldn't let Death get away with a thing,
tore the rotting bark off stricken trees
with that box-cutter beak, eating its weight in beetles.

And there it is, they say, still
sounding off like a factory whistle – *Work, work,*
the day has come – still excavating caves in deadwood,
flashing red, white and black
through the gloom of old-growth bogs.

And you, mother,
oh Lord God how you come and go in the dismal dark!

NATIVITY

I arranged them eleven years ago today
like warriors enlisted to grant safe passage
to the world she was being born into:

teak and mahogany shepherds
and Wise Men from Tanzania, tending
to the business of a birth

on a shelf by her barred bed where
she labored and was delivered
into black swaddling for the long trip.

Her army vanished soon after, but must
have allowed her to travel in good spirits
for she's been in touch from time to time.

The shepherds and magi surfaced
today, unswaddled from brown paper
wrappings, good as new and she with them,

reaching over unsteadily past the bars
of her bed to cradle the child, ensuring
long life and in the end, rebirth.

HEDGEHOG

It's late February, your favorite month.
The Redwings are back early this year
and for no reason a wooden hedgehog,
that children's toy atop a small ramp
I brought back for you from Bohemia
and reclaimed when you went elsewhere,
just clicked down its wooden hill
as if to find water after long hibernation.
How the clicking sounded like your heels
passing my room after a long night out.

Selections from

LEARNING THE ANGELS

THE OTHER WOMAN

She's no beauty, I'll tell you – gaps
in her teeth, game leg, foul breath.
But some personality!

And ubiquitous?
I'll be on the town with the wife
when a trash can lid,
a manhole cover
will budge, and there she'll be.

Right off she'll have me
cruising with alligators
in the sewer system, inspired
by loss – wish bone, pope's nose,
the pith and rind of things.
She introduces me
to glamor – a dime in the gutter,
a glitter in the slime.

Or this. I'll be on a cruise with
the little woman, not a thing amiss
(plaid pants, polo shirt)
when a strange bird with that
frizzed hair and green walleyes of hers

will have me
looping, diving, bombing the QE II,
the layers and layers
and lacework and frosting of her

and at the top in a candy bower
the little bride, the little groom.
We laugh and laugh,
my Muse and I.

THE RISING

After love it is good,
the sun just up,
to place apple or birch
on the embers, breathe

in, sit silent with you,
and look
out the west window
to the swamp maple

catching the first
salmon light
in its highest winter-
white branches.

Today, a violet blush
rises up the trunk
and limbs —
wave on wave of it.

Though we know
it's shadows of smoke
from the wood stove,
we also know better.

DREAMING IRENE

Dense fog at dawn,
high seas, South Beach
rebuilt last night
and nothing quite
itself.

That cairn of clothing
topped off with briefs
is what's left of me.

I sprint,
I scallop the sand,
bank left, bank right,

right into Irene Wade
from down the beach
who breasts the wind,
her breasts all out,
her fur that curly it's
a crime.

What to do
is jump the surf,
my sprit, her jugs
so much in sync
we laugh like kids

until behold, we fall
to our knees,
one craft,
she fore, I aft.

THE REVEREND CHARLES WADSWORTH
GOES BIRDING WITH EMILY DICKINSON

In the heart of your woods (you white as bloodroot,
  I decently black
but for the streak of my cleric's collar), "How various
  the thing with feathers,"
you quip, and introduce me to the *which-a-ta which-*
  a-ta which of a black-masked blur of gold

you label the Bandit Bird. Now the hollow near-
  and-far thrumping
of a grouse – as if through the soles of my feet – feels
  like a quicker bumping of the blood,
and you settle your hand on my shoulder. Around us
  the underworld

declares itself in three-bladed trillium – "the Trinity
  Flower,"
you say, "a finery the decadent earth gives rise to" –
  and show me where
its white turns pink, almost mauve. I touch the hand
  you touch me with.

TWO LADIES WALTZING

after "A Summer Night" by Winslow Homer

We are the dancers you placed upon
a midnight promontory
to waltz, moon-washed, to the bang, lap and
whisper of surf, the swish and snap
of taffeta. Small wonder our careful hair has

come undone and our dance taken
a turn you deplore. Are we more immoral
than the shudder of gold
you lavish on the muscling sea? It does no good
to double the ply of our gowns

and slow the dance, arrange our hair in buns.
Revised, our thighs are all
the more Grecian
for the cling of their apparel.
What's taffeta taut with wind but celebration

of taffeta's dismantling!
Don't scowl so, mister. You made me
close my eyes, nestle my chin on her shoulder,
brush my lips across the tender
of a hand — hers, mine, no matter,

and made our joined
hands reach for the precipice
not for balance but to court vertigo,
fingers tracing fingers so lightly they shiver
like the brush you would cancel us with and can't.

SLOW DANCE, VILLEJEAN

After an untitled photograph by Gilles Peress

It's fall in the photo, late fall in fact, judging
by the shriveled leaves on this cul-de-sac's
deserted hardpan littered
with trampled cartons, tin and sheetrock.

The roadside trees, bare now, are overgrown
with vines. Nailed to the trees, a few boards
dangle, out of kilter,
the last of childhood's rungs.

Center right is a Citröen with a hint of fins,
circa 1957, and leaning against it
a battered Mobylette.
On the horizon a factory blocks the sky,

but what a camera's depth of field brings in
is forgotten behind the closed eyes
of the couple in the foreground.
She is short, stout, thick-ankled — and he

not much taller, chin receding,
face discolored jaggedly from neck to temple.
Her hand, loose on his rough wool sweater
over the heart,

is pressed by his. He has his other hand
around her waist, and each has one foot
forward, one back. Their down-turned brows
are touching. He hums their song.

BLUES IS NOT THE WORD FOR IT

Her blood has gone bad, plasma cells proliferating,
hounding the whites and reds, driving them out,
infiltrating bones, marauding the marrow, rendering
it soft as sponge. Limbs and fingers break casually.

For months he's stood guard. Today, advised to ease
his vigil, go fishing, he finds himself beyond the mouth
of Boston Harbor, the tide ebbing, Devil's Back rising
out of the sea like something Cretaceous.

Hundreds of terns line the island's spine, waiting.
Now a distant roiling of water. The terns begin
to circle, and the roiling quickens to Bluefish
launching themselves, slicing the air gray and purple,

tossing bloodied small fry to the gold of late afternoon.
They vanish in a hurtle of terns, many falling back to
Blues cornering them against the flank of Devil's Back
in a radiant fury of feasting, voracious as malignancy.

With each cast he hauls in a two-foot Blue,
dodges its knife-edged fins, hammers the head, rips out
the hook with pliers, casts again, shifts from left to right-
handed reel. At dusk, with so many Blues piled high,

he's done, tosses them, heads home. Passing the mouth
of the harbor, he's deafened by a Delta roiling the water
just short of touchdown at Logan, nearly swamping him.
Landing lights rake the boat like radiation.

Then the sanity of the inner harbor. He calls her cell,
says "Blues is not the word for it."

PENDERGAST'S GARAGE

after "Gas," Edward Hopper

It's 1940, dusk. There are bats
over Pendergast's Garage, and Mr. P
is polishing a pump.
His coveralls are neatly pressed.

Beyond him, rest room signs grow dim –
no Women, no Men. Lights come on,
illuminate Milky Ways, Mars Bars,
maps of six states and Essex County.

A part of the sky is still on fire.
It turns the growth along Pine Road
(to which Mr. P has his back) bright
red, and deeper red the Flying Horse

big-thighed on the Mobil sign,
which hangs like a flag, and on each
bubble-headed pump and crossing
the heart of Mr. Pendergast.

Once, he knew the beast to mount,
straight up, the dark
above the thickening trees. Now he's
happy to polish, sees himself in a pump.

HOMECOMING

*Homer has Penelope ask her maid to move the marriage
bed, though one post of it is a rooted tree, in order to be
sure Odysseus, just back from war and roaming, is not an
impersonator. The real story may be quite different.*

After so much waiting for him,
weaving a vision of his hands, gentle
in my hair, on my nape,
down the narrows of my waist,
and afterwards unweaving, tearing him
out, thread by thread, from my heart,

he shows up, grizzled by years
of war, in time to see me choose another.
Then the massacre of suitors, piling up
of bodies still twitching like breathless fish,
and the servant girls
who haven't saved themselves for him

stripped and strung up one by one
to dance on air. Stink of blood and urine.
A little scrubbing and strewing of rush
will erase it, he says. Then it's time –
roast sucklings, harp and dulcimer,
tasseled bellies dancing . . .

When he holds out his hands, I understand
the dance he has in mind. I'm not one of his
adventures. When he says it's time for the
marital bed, I say he can have it to himself –
I'll see the bed is moved where he wants.
And he rages like a child, brandishes

a lecture: how he built his house around
an olive tree carved and polished until
it was good enough to be a corner post
of the master bed, immovable . . .
On and on before I reoccur to him.

Shall I lie, say the bed won't budge?
I severed it myself, I tell him. I tell him
what else has been lost, what else cut off
which bled at every knot, remembering.

THE USE OF SONG

for W. B. Yeats

So he married Georgie, settled down
in a stone tower restored for her.
She was not his first
choice or his second, and thus

was savage in her claim to be beyond
mere choice. The others, she said,
could damn well keep their distance.

Beyond the tower, rebellion turned
to civil war, the dead
accumulated in streets and fields,
the spring runoff ran red.

Halfway up the tower's spiral stairs

in a nook for Norman archers,
a deep-piled nest of spattered sticks,
bleached bone and clumps of fur was
full of what he called *passionate intensity*.

As he passed it on his way
to the parapets, what hurled itself full-
fledged at the sky, its wings swept back,
might as well have been a Norman
arrow meant for the Irish rabble.

In the nest young kestrels fought
for what was left of that day's rabbit
and headless rodent.

When he ranted against such fury,
too much the fury of the world beyond,
his bride suspected he meant her own,
which she thus unleashed at him.

It was enough to send him to his den
where his familiar parrot's repertoire
commended song
for one so caught in the cage of history.

He survived by turning
the worst in woman, man and beast
to verse.

APOLOGY

Sasha Tolstoy to Count Leo

At 82 you were still going strong.
Mother waited for you to blurt out
your lover's name while you dreamed,
and she spent long afternoons rooting
in your diary, letters, crumpled notes.

One last time, I saw you go, kept still –
until I heard who this love was
and had to track you down. For her part,
never played better, mother followed
with her maids and doctor and secretary
on a private train.

We found you stricken at a railway depot
involved in your last affair.

Mother did the Widow-to-be
and ordered the Abbot to exact from you
a public apology to God
for all your lusts and now this final folly.

I locked her out of your room, locked
everyone out. But when you grew delirious
and raised an invisible pen
to write it all down on the air,

I let in the specialist sent by mother,
let you be strapped to the bed
so camphor and morphine could have

their way, let the black balloon of oxygen
breathe into you, fit to muffle the animal cry
you longed for, the culmination.

At the end, when a foolish nurse closed
your eyes, slicked down your wild white hair,
parted it on the wrong side, and stitched
your mouth shut, I didn't scream at her,
didn't knock her hand away,

didn't hurl myself at mother when she burst in
and knelt by you for the whirl
of a newsman's camera.
I was that civilized. Forgive me, Papa.
No, don't.

A PAIR OF HOPPERS

1. *Office at Night,* Edward Hopper, 1940

Stop putting on airs, sir.
It's not the annual report that keeps you
at your desk so late.
I do.

As you see, Hopper's made improvements
in me. I am, you'll agree, more
bosomed and buttocked.

Don't tell me you don't get it,
the way I ease a file drawer open,

lick a finger, curl my tongue around it,
run it down your ridged
folders, and with a sort of pistol

crack
from one high heel, pin
the balance sheet blown off your blotter.

Your options are down to one, mister.
You think there's always the cold mouth-
piece of the phone
to call the wife to say you're on the way?

Fat chance. In no time I'll kneel
to pick up your Profits & Losses and
find your eyes on the valley of my cleavage.

You won't be in any position to tell me
my *Yours Truely* is misspelled.
The only truth is the whisper
of rayon on nylon.

2. *Hotel by a Railroad,* Edward Hopper, 1952

Not satisfied? After thirty years of forgetting
I *am* your wife? Look at you, some stiff staring
out the open window Hopper has left open as if
it might be just the ticket.

The few hairs still sticking to your skull are shades
of your threadbare flannels.
The only things not gray about you

are the little red tip of your fag
and those bloodshot eyes squinting at what –
the rails? As if you had the guts to ride them or,
God help you, jump.

So what is it? Let me guess.
You're staring at that opening across the tracks,
thinking

the sun rising precisely between Acme Auto Parts
and the High Meadow Funeral Home
means today's the day for one last adventure.
Some Druid you are!

Button your fly, Don Juan, and look behind you.
From here I can see through those
moth-eaten socks

your heels
won't be growing any wings. How dreary the news
of your comings and goings
in the black little book on my lap.

Are you blind? Look, your bed is made. There,
laid out on that pale face of a pillow, mister,
your spectacles.

BRINK

This April the winter is too much
with us, has closed love's loopholes.

True, the amaryllis gaudy on its sill
has put out all its scarlet trumpets,
no, not trumpets — loudspeakers,

the kind you see back to back
at political rallies aimed all four ways,
making promises. Now this ruckus
by the forced forsythia. What's up

is a snake from the crawl space
taking a stab at the dog,
pink gums blossoming. It misses
and misses. The dog dances in and out
like the tongue of the snake.

It's enough of a game to give us heart,
tell us to head for the river.
From a sun-struck bank we discover
a turtle basking, red and yellow
neck erect, and there, a mallard riding
a mallard.

Where better for love, lady, than here
upon the brink?

Selections from

AN ASTONISHMENT
AND AN HISSING

I AM

I am

the hiss of stars,
outrageous flame
that made from naught
the Zygote, the Aardvark.

I am

the throaty dark,
the belly of Leviathan,
the holes in space
that swallow light.

RAVEN

*Noah opened the window of the ark which
he had made. And he sent forth a raven,
which went forth to and fro.* — Genesis, 8

Call me Raven.
The dawn can color the night
all it wants, can inspire

the worst sort of poetry.
No matter.
I'll be all the blacker. Who says

a line's the shortest way? I am.
What's dead ahead
of me's well named. I ram it.

Whatever you want me to do
I won't.
Send me out to find dry land

and home like a dove?
I'll make a home of the sea,
rig a stick with a fake olive leaf

for a pin-headed pigeon to find.
I know the Flood's forever.
I made it.

EVE

Wherever I looked I was fourteen –
in bloodroot cupping the afternoon rain,
in the garden pool I bent above,
in the dew collecting on his nether curls.

The lilac leaves
were hearts that touched and twined
like tongues.
Then that other tongue: *Eat this and learn.*

I meant to know, eased open a fig, pink
and plum and thick as night with seed,

sucked it dry, my face half fig,
and could not stop

until a treeful of skins lay at my feet.
On my fur ripe with juice
wide leaves settled, five-lobed
like hands, his hands awakening me.

AS FOR JOSEPH

Behold I have dreamed another dream and
behold the sun, the moon and eleven stars
were bowing down to me. — Genesis, 37

I say we have no choice. This Joseph
loves his brothers no more than the swine
he dotes on, croons to sleep in mire,
and the buzzards with us in mind.
He calls it all fair game

for poetry. And if he thinks of brothers . . .
Last night, he says, he saw the 11 of us
bow down to him. We saw just a glitter
of wolves beyond the circle of the fire,
no stars. Can the whimsies of a pretty boy

get a barren cow with calf? Or freshen
the udders of our ewes? Would he feast
on dreams
when we must gag on gristle? And sing
of a land whose rivers flood faithfully

when our one good well is dry?
I say we rid ourselves of him. The times
do not allow for poetry.

MIRIAM

Up to her knees in muck,
Miriam wove with rushes, daubed with slime
an ark to save her brother from the law.
Later when young Egyptian thugs dared mimic
his stutter, she took them on.

With Jehovah burning like a furnace in Moses,
who else was fond enough to mourn
a plague's worth of frogs beaten flat as dung,
piled high as monuments, a stench?

When the long march lengthened,
manna spoiling in the desert and Moses
talking forever to his Mountain,
she had her people give their gold –
ten thousand earrings, bracelets, pendants –
to the fire to make the glittering god
who promised wells, ripe olives,
unction for the old whose skin was rags.

In the end, when the people
dancing naked in their joy of the golden calf
were speared like spawning fish by Moses
and his men, and when he set the Cherubim,

winged bulls, on the ark of his jealous god,
Miriam preferred the desert sun,
jackals and buzzards, to men and the gods
of men.

I, MICHAL

*Michal the daughter of Saul looked out of the window and
saw King David leaping and dancing before his Lord; and
she despised him in her heart...and said, "How the king of
Israel honored himself today, uncovering himself today
before the eyes of his servants' maids."*   — II Samuel, 6

I ought to know. I'm Queen here,
I, Michal, daughter of a King,
granddaughter of judges. And I say

David showed what a peasant he was
when he studied Bathsheba in her tub,
perusing her from the palace roof.
And how kingly when our firstborn died
to ride her for birth!

When the Word came out of hiding
to Jerusalem, what royalty to greet It
with cymbals, flutes and tambourines
as if Commandments carved on stone

and fired in the furnace of Yahweh
were dancing girls!
Only a shepherd would have strewn
with flowers the ark that carried

God's Word, and danced like a goat
before It, his manhood free for all
to see. And who else would have sung
to the Lord like a lover?

SHEBA

*King Solomon loved many foreign women: the daughter of Pharaoh,
and Moabite, Ammonite, Edomite, Sidonian, and Hittite women.*
Kings, 11

When Sheba dismounted, I waited
and history stopped
while the Queen of Queens stroked her camel,
spoke gibberish to the beast.

And then – before my golden doors,
my hundred silver harps in unison,
my throne of ivory
and brazen peacocks set with jade and lapis lazuli,
she yawned.

I, Solomon, spoke wisely of peace and war,
described the dimensions of my newest temple,
considered the speed of Syrian chariots
and Sidonian galleys,
was applauded,

and heard from Sheba nothing
but the hiss of sand and wind and serpent.

She slid out quietly one night, faded into desert

with all her train. The watchdogs were silent,
none of my thousand horses neighed.

Since then I have searched for her in the dark
of women from alleys and outlands –
Ammonites, Hittites ... There is revolt, the temple
crumbles. Secret in its sanctuary, I pray
for the hiss of sand and wind and serpent.

AN ASTONISHMENT AND AN HISSING

Babylon shall become heaps, a dwelling place for dragons,
an astonishment and an hissing, without an inhabitant.
– Jeremiah, 51

And it was as the hand had written on her wall:
the Jewel of the East, Lady of Two Rivers,
Ark of Ishtar and Marduk – Babylon

was dust. The wonder of her gardens hung to veil
too flagrant communion from the jealous gods,
her Tower of Towers,

the manacled dragons inlaid along her avenues
and sculpted kings brazen as the bulging sun
that crouched behind the Tigris,

her myriad victories
carved in ivory set in lapis lazuli – all
were broken, all burned.

After the pitch that bound her bricks

ran boiling in the streets, and golden gods, gone
molten, flowed in channels carved for blood,

after the perfumed cedar of ceilings cooled to ash
and even Alexander, kicking through the rubble,
grew weak at the thought of raising her again —

after her shame was all the world could wish,
Jehovah wished more, uncoiled long muscles,
and sinuous as script, slid into her, hissing.

In the end the brown-voiced Euphrates
and wailing siroccos
buried her under centuries of silt and sand,

buried all but the ghost of Nebuchadnezzar.
Ox-bodied, buzzard-clawed, he crawls
the desert over Babylon.

SABBATH NOON IN NAZARETH

That he has her this Sabbath noon
as flour dust settles in his bakery
and dung stinks in a Nazarene alley

is not what Mary had in mind.
Nor is this she sees come over her
beyond his acrid sweat, dank fur —

this darkness risen high above,
hovering,
and descending like accumulated

storm — a serious sky consumed
with interest in the earth, a sky
enough to spark the start

of everything. Now, deep in her
this Sabbath noon in Nazareth,
a sudden shock — *I Am, I Am.*

HEROD

Outraged by John the Baptist's condemnation
of her and seeing that her husband has been
swayed by it, Herod's wife Herodias urges her
daughter Salome to seduce Herod and extract
a promise of John's head.

Among the snakes, the muck
and stench of the Jordan, held under
by the Baptist
longer than the rest, I understood
the lust my love amounted to

and disavowed her slender neck,
her tilted breasts, her sly long legs
and clever feet that toyed with me
beneath the royal banquet table.

From the throne I confessed
her husband's death had been
no accident. I began my penance,
praised the God of the Baptist.

Last night she had her daughter
dance before me,
nipples tasseled, hip bells jangling,
belly swirling lush with oils

and a slender river of amber down
from the small lake of her navel
to the darker sea beneath.
Later the girl begged a thing I gave,

exhausted, half asleep in her lap.
This morning I see it, impaled
on a post of my bed, eyes gouged,
tongue ripped

from the gape of its jaws.
My lady wears the Baptist's teeth
on a braid of his hair, memento
mori, mine.

YOU, SHADRACH

Then Nebuchadnezzar the king was astonished,
and said . . . Lo, I see four men loose, walking in
the midst of the fire, and they have no hurt; and
the form of the fourth is like an Angel of God.
—Daniel, 3

His annunciation the crack of jackboots,
His anthem the rattle of cattle cars
in the dead of night,

His law the thud and probe of lead
in your gut,

this dark God of Job
has melted the gold from your teeth,
washed himself white with the soap
of your flesh,
made parchment of your skin,
put out the sun with the smoke of
your "simplification." As ever, He
twists to strengthen your sinews.

And you, Shadrach
in the heart of the furnace
dance, dance higher than the flames,
your God in your arms.

Selections from

COUNTING TO CHRISTMAS

PRAISE IN DECEMBER

Speak ye well of the meadow mice,
wee things to have weathered
the freeze
with breath enough to spare
to leave a rime like stars
above each burrow in the field.
Bring gifts, bow down, and learn.

WINTER GARDEN

for Sarah

She celebrates solstice
by the river, finds

among spent thistle
and Scouring Reed

a wild asparagus bush
hung with rounds of

tarnished silver pods
and picks a fistful,

some still half red,
so brittle she's careful

not to spill the black
and tear-shaped seed

she carries
to her winter garden.

UNDERWORLD

for my mother

Celebrating the season, she cleaves
the tough-skinned pomegranate
to its succulent center.

The trick's to work the ruby seeds
from their white gold settings,
black market jeweler dismantling

some hot one-of-a-kind.
She pries with the twisted fingers
of her mother

and grand and great grandmother
collecting the sweet pulp of
candy seeds for the Christmas salad.

CHRISTMAS CREEK

hardens
but before going under

for good, it's flashy
midstream, unspools
its reds and pinks

at sunset
like Christmas ribbon.
Where ice meets water
it chimes.

CELEBRATION

A dozen apples in December
shrink and wrinkle, go from dark
to darker, hang by threads
no thicker than our own.
And yet — how like ornaments
a dozen apples in December
and how the sparrows, reeling,
wassail on the earth-gold wine
a dozen apples, aging, brew
beneath a low and southern sun.

NOELING IN THE HOOSEGOW

for Gladys Egdahl Couch

When the church burned down
that December, town hall served.
Rose pumped an old foot-organ so hard
she pounded the floor

above the heads of the drunks
in the lock-up below.
She meant it, was fiercely in favor
of God

but not of how
when *God Rest Ye Merry Gentlemen*
ended, it didn't
in the underworld,

accompanied by banging and jangling
of bars, slurring
into *Away in a Manger* off key
but softly

softly, until Rose played along.
This time she did her pumping gently.
Being six,
I said it was wise men. No one said no.

COUNTING TO CHRISTMAS

At the dark end of the year
when the owl sweet talks
all night, I work the Advent
calendar, open another

door, wait to look in
on the child. Let's hope
I'm not a spy, house to house,
for Herod, or that if I am

I'll quit the service
when I find what I came for.
Now the sweet talk quickens
to silence. What murder is

on the wing? I look for signs
of it in myself — and ask
what gift I have to offer Him
that He should welcome me.

ADVENT

Now
by the last
of the sun

this flight
of gilded
snow

so fine it
has nothing
to do

with earth
swirls
rises

raises
my sights
to a sun-

struck ash
and there
high up

a sign
of nativity:
the sway of

a leaf-and-
twig-knit red
squirrel nest.

SOLSTICE CEREMONY

The lights are out, the fires are cold
in Zuni Pueblo. It is time. Now
across the ice-hard mesa and wash
he comes,

chest and legs dappled red and blue,
blue beads at his wrist and neck,
Redtail feather on a white-spotted hood
and over his shoulder a fawn skin

filled with the rattling sunflower seed.
He carries a torch against
the dark, and reaches the people,
blesses the hearths,

relights the fires,
dances with the cloud-white, nimbus-
headed, cedar-and-bow-bearing Rain
God of the North. The year begins.

CHRISTMAS BAT

An hour till midnight service
and the sexton has fired up the furnace.
What a banging of pipes for Christmas!

Look, a bat abiding in the rafters
is flying low above
the manger. He tips his wings toward

a mite, no doubt from the evergreen.
Something mute, inhuman stirs in me.
I kneel like one of Hardy's oxen,
await the gift

of words. Back and forth in the nave
I hear the shuttle of wings like pages
turning to the proper carol.

MIDNIGHT IN THE BARN

I was nine and waiting
Christmas Eve
for the animals to kneel

and speak. Not to miss
a word, I was early, bearing
apples, carrots, turnips.

I gave my gifts,
I scratched the beasts,
I settled in the straw.

And just at twelve
by the bells from town
the miracle was

I spoke Clydesdale,
I carried on in Lamb.

CHRISTMAS EVE IN CIENFUEGOS

For three days now the fishermen have been
overboard in golden wine, the sweet solera
saved for Christmas time.

This night of nights
their wives, sisters, daughters guide them
past the manger
to the altar rail. The fishermen weep . . .
then go to town
in Jacinto's tuna truck,
singing, oh lord singing and singing —

On Christmas day, on Christmas day
how the fishes will guzzle and the dolphins dance,
dance and guzzle and guzzle and dance . . .

At Ramon's, warming up for what's to come,
the fishermen make bad flamenco.
In jockey shorts and high rubber boots
Juan Lopez leaps like a cod. Such cracks
he makes in stucco walls.
Ramon counts cadence,
snaps his fingers loud as whips.
Jacinto's gift is the hand in his armpit
squeezed and squeezed like an accordion.

Well may the porcelain Christ
above the brand new washbowl
smile. He knows such bad flamenco
is for him. He knows twelve days from now

Juan Lopez, Jacinto and Ramon will sober up
to harness a tractor
to a wagon bright with cherubs and bulls
to pull the terra cotta magi into town.
How little the wise men will totter.

CACTUS, DECEMBER 25

For once the Christmas Cactus is
no misnomer. It's out

for itself, of course. All this purpled red
propositions hummingbirds and honeybees,

whatever has wings
in a room where the only things that do

are bright tin angels on the mantelpiece.
Alas.

Still, what trumpets the cactus lifts
in unison — *Good News, Good News!*

THE ADORATION OF MELCHIOR

The horns of the oxen are gilded
by a lean fire of twigs and dung,
and standing water celebrates

the star. On such a night
I cannot deny a snake the egg

it takes in slack soft jaws

or a rat the corn it steals, in love
with seed.
All things according to their kind

adore. The somber ewes bow down
on gnarled knees. I give my gift
and hold the child like new regalia.

CHRISTMAS

day is done. Wherever the trees
aren't violet on a field of white
they're white on deepening blue.

Carelessly a ribbon red as wrapping
lies along a line of hills.
The opening is done.

What's left to give
is simple as violet on a field
of white.

BLIND BEGGAR, KEY WEST

after Jacob Lawrence, "Beggar No. 1"

Despite the jubilation of the First Baptist's
crèche with its bright inner circle, angels
tooting, and elaborate magi processing,

the gist of the New Year's service is *Repent,*

Repent! I'm dour when I leave,
go a block, and see a procession heading
my way. A half dozen children cavort,
led by a boy waving a flag so many-colored

it blazes white. Red, yellow, violet, blue
getups — oh the Caribbean splendor
of such drummers, kazooers, kite-fliers!
The heart of their parade

is a gaunt tall man in dark glasses, arrayed
in carmine, gold, deep purple and burgundy,
announcing his station with a tapping cane.
He bears the gift of a tin can painted white.

This is the way a wise man comes, asking less
for alms than for me to pull glad rags
from the sad sack of my heart.

GETAWAY

after an early work by Mack Burns, age 4

He crayoned his first crèche in three parts.
All's well at the top — the Firmament is
heavenly blue. But the Sky
is trouble. It's full of what — stars or angels
swarming like a plague of leggy spiders.

Just above the manger is a star burst
from something like a Scud
incoming. Part Three has the Baby Jesus
the size of his parents, his feet and head
protruding from a purple perambulator.

A lush brown, black-haired Mary,
her arms and one leg colored jaggedly,
leans forward as if to wheel the giant baby,
hissing to the blueblood blob of Joseph
"Let's get out of here!"

The space around the shed is fire-orange
except for a – camel? Brown as Mary
and humped high as the ridgepole,
it's kicking a hole in the siding. To knock
sense into Joseph's head? Or show it's

raring to go? Maybe left by a Wise Man
after he informed on the king. But –
shouldn't it be a donkey? A minor mistake.
Thank God for its headstrong headful
of a stall somewhere Herod never heard of.

TWELFTH DAY

Freezing at dawn, I tote corn, suet,
black sunflower seed – 12th Day
gifts, though it's barely day despite

such a frenzy of featherbrains, dun
little corn-crackers, seed-huskers.
Says who? They too were there

at the feet of the Magi, scratching
for gifts of grain, bowing in their way,
in love with day.

Like them, I cock an eye at the sun,
already two degrees farther north,
and lay small branches on the hearth

to heat the flue for the larger fire
to come. I open the draft, kindle
a ribbon of flame, add oak.

Such a gift has traveled far to reach
this hearth and home, has come
from the very dawn of history.

Selections from

NORTH NORTHEAST

FROG DAY

The fen I live by is all a gabble, like ducks.
But it isn't ducks. Some other hosanna.
The scum has begun to bulge, go bug-eyed,

jump like Judgment Day.
And I am less defunct for this, more apt to sing,
feel my muse arising from the muck within.

Lo, her peach of a throat is full
of Spring, and she's begun to croak some code
it's up to me to crack.

SPRING SONG

When winter croaks,
when we see the buds tremendously
to be the buds they've been since summer
and hear the sap's obscenities,
when seeds propel themselves to pop,
there's nothing in Ovid I'm not.

NEW ENGLAND
GREENHOUSE

No goings on here,
not a soft-lipped orchid
or lily loose.
What served as Heaven
has fallen, is glass
the rats translate
to sand.

Those smooth gears
that worked above
with a well-oiled hum
are frozen. What was
a garden

is a whistle for wind,
a scurry.
Snow curls in corners
and rust's half through
with the boiler

from which a sapling
heads strictly
for the clear cut sky.

MAGICIAN

He bows, comes closer than seems safe,
washes his hands with air,
shakes out crisp white cuffs like snow,
bows again, pulls from his hat
as nonchalant as March
coons, possums, one or two small bears,
some whistling swans, the usual,

and from thin air an apple branch
he touches once, twice, plays a trill on
until with the magic we've stood so long
in the cold to see, it simply and suddenly

blooms. For finale he vanishes into
the smile of a child who steps right up,
vanishes like face cards up a sleeve.

WILD GRAPES

Consider these grapes,
the real ones, not the fat ones full of sun
with misty skin like a mooning lover's eyes.
The ones I mean grow honestly
in the shade of the trees they climb.
They're small and dark
like eyes that fix on you in a narrow pass
and know you cold.

SMALL TOKEN

Each time I pass the barn this morning
Hobo has laid out her kill
in a different pose: seduction arranged
and rearranged.

Now the mole is draped
across the flagstone path, stomach-up,
and now laid out in the grass,
feet cocked as if to run, tableau vivant.

Sometimes its star
nose points east and sometimes north.
Like any poet Hobo licks a paw,
considering.

PHEASANT IN THE CRAB

The cats full of winter mouse
doze in the barn
& a late sun gilds the glass
behind which I am
like something on display
a curiosity

watching
what declares itself
with hoarse & rusty iambics

come out of the woods
& start & stop
in bronze
white collar
tan spots
red mask

& start
past maple shadows
on the snow
careful
careful now
like anyone skipping cracks
on a sidewalk

& approach the crab apple
as if no candy's hanging
& look anywhere
but at the lowest branch

check left
right
& make an awkward leap
like a boy with his eye
on a Delicious
just beyond him

& pinch a crab & more
where that comes from
then jump to the branch
to settle down
to business.

DAWN ON THE ALLEGASH

for Margy

Like dreams half remembered,
orb webs that bellied all night like sails
are suggested at dawn by
dint of dewdrops strung concentrically,
then catch the sun, their rigging bright.

Where a creek meets the river, the mist
slowly grows coherent, becomes
a slate-gray Blue Heron, head cocked.

Across the river, as if dimly torch-lit
on a cave wall, head under the current
then hugely up, a crag and waterfall
risen above ghost-curls of surface fog,

a moose stares somewhere beyond
and gangles toward it, rearranging river.

SQUIRREL

for Sibley Watson

I am the beast, I ride the snow, my fire
burns warm within. All you with fangs,

ha! I get from here to there, I cope,
I shiver my tail for a start, and go,

leave all of my shadow behind, and stop,
wait for the shadow I threw to catch on –

then climb my tree so cleverly
I'm always on the side away from thee,

O Death with thy claws and a grin.
I win.

THE BATS

for Gerry Shertzer

Call them more than hangers on,
say they set their bounds like so:
a flight from under the southwest eave
to Salter's oak, thence to the old red maple,
two hundred feet to the barn and back
to the oak: deeds

I duly record, drawing a bead on the bats.
I do not know until I empty the sky
how like small hands
the claws at the peak of Beelzebub's wings,
how fine the down in von Richthofen's ears.

ATHENEUM

Below the banner proclaiming a Rodin exhibit
this outdoor sculpture is so exact it's almost alive:
a tan, white-striped hawk, eyes glaring, razor beak

aimed at me. It is mounted
on a buff, pale blue and pinkly iridescent pigeon
in which its talons disappear. Now the hawk blinks
like a switchblade's click, and shifts its weight.
Nothing else moves. Not the pigeon, not I.

FREEZE

The dog and I are down to each other,
doing our best. She's grown her fur
thicker, my winter coat's on. We've left
the stove to see the moon

eclipsed, its silver rendered nothing
but a rusty cent. Feeling a freeze
coming on, I cover the geraniums,
tote a scuttle of coal to see us through,

lock the door, listen
to the Great Horned call the who's who
soon to be grist
and from the hill, yips rising to a howl

high-pitched and full of teeth.
The dog, all ears and nose, ruff up,
growls low in her throat. In light
of the black hole at the heart of our

heavenly spin, I treat the dog to a bone,
stoke the stove with bits of fossil.
In the fire-door, twin eyes
of isinglass glow.

CAT

My teacher's a calico cat. She researches
a haunt of hers, tastes a spot of dry blood
left over from a prodigal kitten

with broken bones for a head, a mouthful
of suckling worms.
She looks into nooks, finds nothing,

recalls the rest of the litter, jumps a tail,
piles on, plays ball with them
to celebrate their lives.

GATHERING

The Monarchs illuminating the gold leaf
of a seaside maple, preparing for migration,
rising up, riding the wind, signing the air
red, black & white, about to go from here
to there in the Valley of Mihoacán,

will not be back. Beyond, wind surfers rise
in their stirrups, wet-suited,
black and bug-like, legs wide, knees bent,
working many-colored transparent sails
in loops and lines. Such a cursive

can't last: storm clouds move in. Still,

I take heart, short-timer myself, admire
the embossing on empty horseshoe crabs
and the bright wrack of washed up shells
where worms worked their insignia

gaudily from inside out before they lost
touch. How utterly all of us
passing through
would leave our mark, saying *I, even I*
was at the gathering.

DAVID DYING

The Shunammite lies like warm earth
on David coldly dying, shrinking
to bone, to simple seed.

She throws her thick black hair
over what she wills to rise
to dance

on air, like David naked before the Ark,
leaping to trumpets and timbrels
to praise the Lord his God.

The Shunammite warms
the spirit whose ark of flesh once loved
Bathsheba bathing open as a water lily.

She lies like warm earth
on David coldly dying
and his soul is as a locust stirring.

JIM'S GARAGE

Sunset declares for Jim's Garage,
congratulates the cracks
in every pane

and turns the blues
(a cloud of exhaust, a bottle
of windshield solvent,
a pool of oil, and Jim himself
in coveralls for a front end job)
to gold.

Hung on the wall, dented hubcaps
(Packard, Hudson, Studebaker)
shine like shields.

ILLUMINATION NIGHT

The children, like angels amok,
have designs on the night underscored by
barooming from the Oak Bluffs bandstand.

They sign the dark with crazed light-sticks,
toss them like burning batons,
barely notice

the lanterns hung from Victorian porches,
hundreds of pleated parchment globes,
but fall silent when —

to an amplified tap from the conductor
at *sea to shining sea* — the lanterns are lit
to illuminate their other worlds

where spaciously the saffron herons soar,
the impossible butterflies blossom and
legendary mammals carry on,

civilizing, for a moment, the children.

THE FLOWER MAN

walks humped
as if his head's too heavy for
its stalk. Truth is

he has bent above so much
so long
he walks the way he works.

He banks his place with leaves
and winters like a root.
A curl of smoke is all.

Then the smoke dies back and
he's up before skunk cabbage
can uncoil,

his tractor's mutter
better news
than any gaggle going north.

TREE MAN

Jacob can have his ladder,
angels, the whole business.
Give me any day the man
with gaffs on his boots

who works his way up
a hundred feet of locust,
chain saw hanging behind
like a monkey's tail.

Give me a man suspended
by faith
in cinch and line,
a man who stands on air

with the sun at his back,
does what he can
and drops down to earth
by a single strand.

HARRY NOBLE

has gone fishing, sweet-talks
trout, reels in, works the hooks
slowly out, no rips, jaws going
like theirs, and throws them back
or more properly

launches them in shallows,
launches all but the woebegone

who wear a sort of rusty fungus
the shape of hands. "Never touch
a trout dry-handed," he says.

With others who work the creek,
the minks, the otters and coons,
he knows his place
and spends good fishing time
on all fours in the mud,

searching for a snarl of line
he's dropped where one of them
may be the worse for it.
"There's snares enough," he says,
"without my own."

PETER FARR

What with a sign reading *Farrs*
Slawter & Taxydurmy,
headless chickens draped on crates,
sheep pelts caked with blood
spread out on bushes to dry, parts
of pick-ups and tractors everywhere,
so little yard
the hens can barely get around,

people talk. What they don't know
is how the night before he kills
he serves whatever is in for it
molasses in its feed
and how he'll croon a steer
halfway to sleep

before he pulls the trigger.

His killing shed steams with innards,
teems with pig head, sheep shank,
smells like cows
birthing.

Once I dreamt he took one of these,
one of those,
built a beast no one had ever seen
and named it, sent it on its way.

So much for dreams. But it is true
he makes it his business
to rebuild the dead.
With wire and batting,
some plaster of Paris, a little glass,

dead owls, dead fox and pickerel
come up bright eyed, fit to kill.

SHE

goes up the dying pine, cuts
quickly from the top down,
chain saw in one hand,
tree in the other,

gives the big rat snake
after eggs in the coop
a boot,
swings a hen around her head
and snaps its neck,

tackles the ram, sits him up,
fleeces the beast
before he comes to.

Evenings, she embroiders
dog-tooth, paintbrush, ragwort.
Her fingers
dart like hummingbirds.

CARRIE WOLF

She was a disgrace, kept hogs in her cellar
and chickens everywhere.

Nights, she rocked on her porch with a .22,
the better to get a bead on the varmints
gnawing her pea patch, and children too.

Out-of-season things grew.
It wasn't right. Come May, her chestnut
looked like Christmas, and we knew

why. Any day they'd hang her from it,
a witch who had it coming when we heaved
the worst we had at her on Halloween.

And what she did
when she caught us filching the biggest
luckiest nuts her chestnut grew,

what she did
was give us sacks and a helping hand
and –

Carrie, that was fine burlap
you saved for us. You shouldn't have.

EIGHT FEET TALLER THAN A WORM

He was eight feet
leaning akimbo back, roaring over
things like the men on the moon.

He lasted three days
before his arms fell off,
his laugh went out
with his bad black teeth
& the sun in a rush unbuttoned him.

His carrot of a nose began to sag
around the sixty-fifth hour,
after which it was all over,
body all but disappearing last night,
head smashed to bits, the old story.

Now he's back where
he began: snowball, stones & a carrot.
The snow will melt tomorrow
& some rabbit will eat the carrot

when we're not looking.

In spite of which he was eight feet
taller than a worm & had his laugh.
Let's hope they say as much for us
when we've gone underground.

OSCAR

for Oscar Egdahl

He was where stove-length
maple, birch, black locust
came from,

the reason
potbellieds glowed
like Ida Reds, Rome Beauties.

You should have seen
his Belgians steam down
Grand Avenue. Their brasses
multiplied the sun.

And how he cut up winter,
stacked great chunks of it
in the icehouse,
wrapped it in sawdust,

he was that sure of summer.

And will not die himself
though dead these thirty years.

The past is a shed
for seasoning, an icehouse
full to the roof,
the place to pass dog days.

SMITH

Outside, ice hung from the eaves.
The land was hard
as the ploughshares and pitchforks

he forged where so much heat
made iron supple as summer
and the old man's muscles worked
like water building over boulders.

All winter, his last, he hammered
and bent, bellows breathing heavily.
As ever the elements were winning.

Ploughshares and pitchforks
were his answer.

CHRISTMAS EVE, CUERNAVACA

for Sah at 5

Part pig, part dragon, this thing:
some thirty helium balloons strung together,
all colors, so pleasantly monstrous
we buy it for you in the zocalo, Christmas Eve.
It fills the van, bouncing from one to another
of us, obscuring the road. When we reach the inn
where there's no room for it
to fit through the door, you smile serenely
and send it sailing – into the manger of the sky.

BREATHING

for Robin

1

All night they were alive, bearing names
he'd slowly read and given breath
in the West River graveyard.

All night they rose
like fog from the bottom,
sighing, and a little too much like family.

Which is why at cockcrow he is up and
dancing on the graves, casting his
own long shadow over the sinking shades.

2

A sudden cold so much it stings our eyes
is why there's all this mist
and why my son has in mind
an argument against his fear that this time
winter is for good:

"The earth is breathing, like me, on the sky,"
he says, and blows a cloud to prove he is
and calls on me to do the same.
He makes enough of us to prove
that if we are the only living things around,
we'll do. And anyway, he says, we aren't.
This mist's from mice and rabbits
and every thing that outlives winter.
Which may be wishful, but when was truth
enough to get us through?

YOUR TIME

for El

Pumpkin moon.
The fields reveal what they've been
up to all summer: grapes and apples
rounded out, seeds more

& more themselves. The sky's ripe
with milkweed sailing

thick as pollen. The burst pods

lean like cocked ears.
I cock my own, press my head to
the swell of your belly.

A COUNTRY DEATH

for Christina Olson

Her heart has stopped banging about;
a jackhammer rattles her frozen plot.

And here in her kitchen where no one
has lit a fire to warm his bones

a line of snow across the floor
is pointing from the door

to her geraniums
and by them, taking the sun,

the rocker I see her riding,
impatient with such civilizing

in the best room where they have her
laid out where she never was at home.

Who else will see the fire is stoked,
the back door filled with oakum?

BONES

for David Rodgers

Wing bones hung from rafters
swing sedately. Horseshoe crabs
and horseshoe crabs are stacked
in a corner

and what those ribs
are doing in the sink, God knows.
Tide by tide, memento moris
multiply. His place has turned

so white
the lips, pearl pink, of a conch
seem obscene. And there
in the dining room,

a whale, its man-long jaw
laid out on the table, its bones
all properly boxed
and tagged with labels reading

Hello, my name is _____
numbered from 1 to 676.
My name is Bones. What's Yours?

ELEGY FOR A RAILWAY MAN

for Jocie

You can put your ear
to his chest,
mister, hammer his heart
with your fist. No one's home.

He's gone, sitting pretty
in the cab of the Silver Queen,
stoking her,
doing 90, maybe 95
between Batavia and Buffalo —

> *Jesus it's sweet to feel her*
> *open up and wail like that*
> *from Churchville to Depew*
> *so lonely, so loco*
> *whatever bays the moon*
> *for miles around*
> *stops to listen*

> *and her sparks alive*
> *as far as Cheektowaga*
> *streaming back like my hair*
> *like the wail of the Queen*
> *like her banner of smoke.*

Heaven's a roundhouse, I say.
I see him clearly
pulling in,
all headlight and old-time fire.

IN CONCLUSION

for Lib, 1907-2000

Their heads and shoulders hover
like clouds, some bright,
some dark. I hear the mourning
in their bedside manners,

cannot tell them
I am dumb with delight,
going on ten, going for the mail,
curling my double-jointed big toe

around small stones,
wishing on each and letting fly
at trees and telephone poles,
then dipping the big tin pail

in the well
and drinking
until my teethe ache, seeing
myself surrounded by sky.

The water tastes of cedar, of moss.
Now the clouds move in,
the small insistent buzz of summer
diminishes. . .

THE RELEASE

for Naomi, 1932-1999

All around me loved ones
are turning pale
as if their life support
has been removed.

Far off, I hear them say
their blessings and goodbye,
goodbye.
There is nothing I can do

for them. I'm six again
and down with measles.
It's dark, curtains
drawn. Now a single ray

shines from the door
where Father's hands enter,
cupping what
they slowly release – wings

so pale a green they're all
but white, floating down
the ray to my open hand,
palm up. How light

the wings. They open, shut
and open, releasing me.

NOTES

Page 12, "Easter Saturday." The *Hyla crucifer* or "peeper" bears a dark cross on its back, much as a crucifer carries the cross in a religious procession.

Page 15, "Dance." In days of yore, a king was liable to be deposed or killed if judged impotent. The Shunammite was a test David's son Adonijah thought he would fail. When the king "knew her not," Adonijah made preparations to depose his father but was unsuccessful, perhaps because the old king knew the Shunammite in an untraditional way. For David's dancing, see the note on "I, Michal" (p. 328).

Page 16, "After the First Hard Frost of Fall." See the note for "Easter Saturday" (p. 12) concerning the "Crucifers."

Page 18, "Nochebuena." The posada ceremony recorded here is a childhood tradition on Nochebuena (Christmas Eve) in various parts of the world, chiefly Mexico, Guatemala and parts of the Southwestern United States.

Page 38, "Pablo's Cello." The parts of a cello have nicely human names.

Page 39, "That First Night." When exposed to the elements, the lacquer coating on the Terra Cotta Warriors guarding the tomb of Qin Shihuangdi dried and flaked off within four minutes, taking with it the brilliant paint beneath. Chemists are attempting to find a way by which archaeologists can prevent this decomposition when they unearth the many still-buried warriors.

Page 48, "Song." For refusing to censor his pen, the poet Ovid was exiled by Emperor Caesar Augustus to an island in the Black Sea.

Page 51, "Going On." American Elms still grow to small and stunted versions of their former glory. They die before reaching maturity. Even in its limited incarnation, the elm is one of the first trees to come into flower, with floral bud-swelling often starting during the first warm days of January and continuing into early February. The elm's maple-like seedpods sail to the ground in late February and early March.

Page 56, "Aubade." Two incidents in the life of Jacob are conflated here: his wrestling with God (or His angel) so victoriously that his opponent is forced to dislocate Jacob's hip, and a vision of angels ascending and descending a heavenly ladder after a night spent by Jacob with his head resting on a rock, "Jacob's Pillow." On both occasions Jacob may have had a bad night, since he was guilty and fearful, having stolen his brother Easu's birthright. As for that bird with its liquid, ascending and descending song, it's a Wood Thrush, whose song is one of the loveliest of any bird's and can be translated as an ascending "Are you there?" and a descending "I am here." I agree with Marianne Moore that imaginary gardens need real toads.

Page 59, "Visitation." Migrating Monarchs fly thousands of miles to "The Valley of the Monarchs" in Mexico, some even making one leg of a return trip. They "ride the thermals," much as hawks do, catching the updraft of a thermal and coasting from its apex to the next updraft. Let's hope the Monarchs survive the destruction of their habitat and the milkweed they depend upon.

Page 62, "Postpartum Depression." Don Marquis once quipped that publishing a book of poetry is like dropping a rose petal into the Grand Canyon and waiting for the echo.

Page 62, "Intervals." The dramatis personae are Miles Davis, Billie Holiday (Lady D), Lester Young, Sonny Rollins, John Coltrane (Trane), and Charlie Parker (The Bird). Birdland was a fabled jazz spot in New York City.

Page 64, "Bernini's Angel." Bernini created ten marble angels to line the Ponte Sant'Angelo. Each carries one of the "instruments of the Passion," objects associated with Christ's Crucifixion. He began with clay models.

Page 66, "A Living." Manatees were mistaken for mermaids or Sirens by early sailors, hence the name of their zoologial order, *Sirenia*. For his part, Odysseus was so aware of the seductive powers of the Sirens that when his ship passed their territory, he had his men tie him to the mast and place beeswax in their ears. After passing through the Straits of Messina, where the Sirens are said to have performed, he continued on toward Ithaka.

Page 68, "Naming." Higgs Field is an energy field containing the Higgs Boson (or "God Particle"). As pure energy passes through the field at the speed of light, it is slowed to the point that it becomes tangible matter. Without the Higgs Field, there would be no you, no me, no bird or beast.

Page 69, "Ito-san and the Tsunami." The poem is based on a *New York Times* story that appeared after the tsunami that devastated northern Japan in 2011.

Page 81, "Crooked Man, Crooked Mile." The Big Dipper is part of Ursa Major (the Great Bear); the handle of the Dipper doubles as the tail of the Bear. The whole of the "Crooked Man" jingle is as follows: "There was a crooked man, and he walked a crooked mile. / He found a crooked sixpence upon a crooked stile. / He bought a crooked cat, which caught a crooked mouse, / And they all lived together in a little crooked house."

Page 99, "Sleeping Giant." The phrase "rip a ditch to pour the enemy Atlantic" is from Donald Hall's poem "The Sleeping Giant."

Page 105, "Dowser." Dowsing allows a person with keen sensory instincts to locate buried objects, not just water: anything from hidden treasure to lost jewelry and buried bodies, which have often been located by dowsers. No "witching wand" is necessary: the witching is within.

Page 139, "End of the Season." Snapping Turtles, which reach prodigious sizes and ages, are surprisingly affable in the water (though not on land, where they are vulnerable). When they take their siestas, lying just under the surface, they will allow a slow-boater to sidle up and scratch their shells with a paddle. Perhaps they like the scraping of the stiff vertical algae growing on their shells.

Page 146, "The Raising." A common saying in ancient Rome, often repeated by Cato, was "Carthago delenda est" (Carthage must be destroyed), since that beautiful North African city-state stood in the way of Rome's imperial designs.

Page 166, "Last." Every fourteen days another language dies out.

Page 172, "Sister Marie Angelica Plays Badminton." The catalyst for this poem was David Inshaw's painting "The Badminton Game."

Page 175, "Riding the Tire." A nod to J. Alfred Prufrock's lovesong.

Page 180, "After Waterloo, What." Many historians believe that Napoleon was murdered by his wine steward, who was in league with the British general charged with preventing Napoleon's escape from the desert island of St. Helena. The speculation is that over a period of time enough arsenic was added to Napoleon's wine to cause a death whose origin could not be detected. The evidence includes an extraordinary amount of arsenic in hair samples taken from Napoleon, as well as his bloated condition during the weeks before his death and the surprising lack of bodily decay found when he was exhumed for burial in France, which has been attributed to the preservative property of arsenic, which is also referenced in "On the Rotting of Apples" (p. 11).

Page 194, "Valentine." James Merrill was fascinated by the voices that spoke through the movement of a planchette on his ouija board.

Page 210, "The Testing." During World War Two, special Italian units were charged with killing Germans posing as Allied infantrymen on the Italian front. Members of those units would leap into foxholes at night and slit the throats of any whose dog tags had the smoothly elliptical shape of the German type.

Page 211, "Beast in the Attic." The beast was, in fact, a pine marten, a member of the weasel family even more ferocious than its cousin, the notorious North American fisher cat.

Page 212, "The Collecting." Sea turtles are unable to retract their heads, which makes it possible to rope their necks.

Page 223, "First Snow in the Garden of the Geishas." The traditional indoctrination of geishas was demanding and their initiation highly ceremonial. They were expected to master not only the art of love but also the arts of dance, theater, poetry and music. The instrument most often played by geishas has always been the shamisen, a long-necked stringed instrument.

Page 224, "Serving Girl with Gallants." Pieter de Hooch began his interior scenes with a pattern of checkered floor tiles in order to create perspective.

Page 226, "Sheep of Pentecost." In the Christian calendar, Pentecost, occurring on the fiftieth day after Easter, marks the occasion when "a rushing mighty wind" filled the house where the Apostles gathered and felt "cloven tongues of fire" descend on them, filling them with the Holy Spirit.

Page 230, "Bruegel's Players." References to the Spanish fortress, the commandeering of firewood, and starvation derive from the occupation of the Lowlands by Hapsburg forces at the time when Pieter Bruegel the Elder was active as a painter. Like this one, many of his works were implicit or explicit protests against the occupation (e.g., "The Massacre of the Innocents," in which Herod's soldiers, sent to slay all male children of two years or less, are clearly Hapsburg cavalry). Even the Lowland spelling of Bruegel's name, from which he dropped the "h," was an act of defiance.

Page 232, "Henri Raymond Marie de Toulouse-Lautrec-Montfa." As a boy, Toulouse-Lautrec broke both of his thigh bones, and because of a genetic disorder, his legs failed to grow, leaving him dwarfed, though his torso and head were normal. It is said that he had hypertrophied genitalia.

Page 236, "Rain Dance." The narrator refers to pre-Anasazi pictographs in the "Grand Gallery," a shallow alcove 150 feet long in what is now called Horseshoe Canyon, located in a remote area of Utah. These pictographs are the most extensive yet discovered.

Page 241, "Arrangements in Blue & Gold." No act by James McNeill Whistler was more outrageous than his creation of the "Peacock Room" in the London town house of Frederick R. Leyland, a wealthy shipowner from Liverpool. It stood in stark contrast to Whistler's lyrical "nocturnes," created at about the same time.

Page 244, "Under the Sun." Tycho Brahe, one of two cosmologists (the other being Johannes Kepler) at the court of Rudolph II in Prague, combined Ptolemaic and Copernican astronomy. He announced that the sun revolved around Earth while all the other planets revolved around the sun.

Page 274, "Lair of the Word." Legend has it that St. Jerome befriended a lion during his years of isolation in a Syrian desert. He apparently allowed the legend to grow.

Page 280, "Company." In earlier times, illiterate recruits were taught to tell their left from their right feet by tying hay to one and straw to the other. Sergeants would bark "Hay foot, straw foot" instead of "Left, right." The marching song quoted here is part of a vast body of bawdy music safely stored in the memories of drill sergeants everywhere.

Page 282, "In Touch." See the note for "End of the Season" (p. 139).

Page 284, "Your Things." The game of marbles referred to is the one that is played "for keeps": winning players get to keep the marbles of the losers, who have "lost their marbles."

Page 290, "Get Used to Endings." The black swans of Martha's Vineyard mentioned in several poems are a strange and wonderful aberration and owe nothing to "Swan lake."

Page 294, "Holding." Lines 7-12 are from "Departure" (*Every Sky,* 2003) by my mother and mentor, Eleanor Atterbury McQuilkin.

Page 309, "The Reverend Charles Wadsworth Goes Birding with Emily Dickinson." When Emily mentions "the thing with feathers," she is referring to Hope.

Page 310, "Two Ladies Waltzing." The poem is based on Winslow Homer's "A Summer Night," which was such a scandal that no American Museum would display it. Only the French would countenance the work. It hangs at the Musée d'Orsay. The artwork on which this poem and others in the book are based can be found on the internet.

Page 315, "The Use of Song." Yeats' sudden marriage to Georgie Hyde-

Lees was tempestuous and clearly second best to what Yeats had hoped for with Maud Gonne and then her daughter. Its analogue, the Irish Civil War, was the catalyst for Yeats' "The Second Coming," in which "The best lack all conviction, while the worst/are full of passionate intensity."

Page 317, "Apology." The poem is based on numerous reports of Tolstoy's last days, which ended at a railway depot as he was escaping the false imprisonment he felt he suffered at the hands of his wife. A few of the details in the poem are based on the semi-fictional novel *The Last Station* by Jay Parini.

Page 326, "As for Joseph." Joseph's story is well known – how his brothers, jealous that he was favored by their father and, one suspects, put off by his dreamy nature, sold him into slavery, dipping in blood the Coat of Many Colors given him by his father and saying he was killed by lions. When in Egyptian bondage, Joseph earned the Pharaoh's favor because of his interpretations of dreams.

Page 327, "Miriam." We know Miriam partly from the way she built the ark that saved her brother, the infant Moses, then convinced Pharaoh's daughter to let him be raised by their mother. Despite her song of joy when the Pharaoh's forces were drowned by the Red Sea, she seems to have had a strong mothering instinct. The Bible says that Miriam's other brother, Aaron, was responsible for the Golden Calf formed to bring relief to the Jewish people, who were suffering terrible deprivation during their exodus from Egypt; but Miriam was very likely the ring-leader, being the more forceful and compassionate of the two.

Page 328, "I, Michal." The story of David and Bathsheba is well known, but somewhat less known is the story of David's dancing to celebrate the arrival in Jerusalem of the Ark of the Covenant carrying the Ten Commandments, which had been hidden for a period of time. Wearing only a loincloth, he cavorted before the Ark so ecstatically that his fearfully proper wife, Michal, was shocked. She was, after all, the daughter of King Saul and had "married down" when she wed a commoner.

Page 332, "Herod." In order to marry Herodias, King Herod arranged to have her husband killed in battle, much as King David did in order to marry Bathsheba. John the Baptist railed against the marriage, incurring the wrath of Herodias, who convinced her daughter, Salome, to seduce Herod and ask for the head of John in payment for her favors.

Pages 341 & 342, "Christmas Bat" and "Midnight in the Barn." In "The Oxen," Thomas Hardy also refers to the legend that at midnight of Christmas Eve, animals kneel. Other versions of the legend give them the ability to speak in order to praise God.

Page 350, "Frog Day." A bogful of Wood Frogs sounds very much like a pondful of mallards.

Page 359, "David Dying." See the note on "Dance" (p. 15).

Page 364, "She." A shearer sits a sheep to be fleeced on its hand quarters, which pacifies it.

INDEX OF TITLES

ABOUT THE AUTHOR

Rennie McQuilkin is the Poet Laureate of Connecticut. His work has appeared in *The Atlantic, Poetry, The Southern Review, The Yale Review, The Hudson Review, The American Scholar, Crazyhorse,* and elsewhere. This is his fifteenth poetry collection. He has received numerous awards for his work, including fellowships from the National Endowment for the Arts and the Connecticut Commission on the Arts, the Ruth Fox Award of the New England Poetry Club, the Swallows Tale Poetry Award, and the Texas Review Chapbook Prize. He has been granted a Lifetime Achievement Award by the Connecticut Center for the Book; and in 2010 his volume of new and selected poems, *The Weathering*, was awarded the Center's annual poetry prize under the aegis of the Library of Congress. For ten years he directed the Sunken Garden Poetry Festival, which he co-founded at Hill-Stead Museum in Farmington, Connecticut. With his wife, the artist Sarah McQuilkin, he lives in Simsbury, CT, where he is the local poet laureate.

North of Eden is set in Perpetua, designer Eric Gill's most celebrated typeface. The clean, chiseled look of this font reflects its creator's stone- cutting work.

To order additional copies of this book
or other Antrim House titles, contact the publisher at

Antrim House
21 Goodrich Rd., Simsbury, CT 06070
860.217.0023, AntrimHouse@comcast.net
or the house website (www.AntrimHouseBooks.com).

•

On the house website
in addition to information on books
you will find sample poems, upcoming events,
and a "seminar room" featuring supplemental biography,
notes, images, poems, reviews, and
writing suggestions.

CPSIA information can be obtained
at www.ICGtesting.com
Printed in the USA
FSOW01n0135070817
37203FS

9 781943 826254